A Critique
D.H. LAWRENCE
Sons And Lovers

Published by
MANTHAN PUBLICATIONS
Opp. University Boys Hostel,
Delhi Road, Model Town,
ROHTAK-124001

A Critique
D. H. LAWRENCE
SONS AND LOVERS

D.S. DALAL

MANTHAN PUBLICATIONS
ROHTAK

Publiser :
MANTHAN PUBLICATIONS
Opp. University Boys Hostel,
Delhi Road, Model Town,
ROHTAK-124001

ISBN 81-85235-23-6

First Edition : 1992

Price : **Rs. 135.00**

Printed at :
Choudhry Printers
Old Moujpur
Delhi 110053.

Dedicated to Dr. Vitthal Dass Modi
for
His Love of Nature
and
Service of Humanity

CONTENTS

INTRODUCTORY

This study aims at showing D.H. Lawrence (1885—1930) in a reasoned out correct critical perspective. In view of the urgencies and requirements of this short-term project, it has been decided to take up Lawrence's *Sons and Lovers* (1913) for the purpose of analysis and exemplification. I have chosen this novel not because I consider it as Lawrence's best work but because it has almost all the cardinal features of his vision and design and also that this project may lead further to an analysis of *The Rainbow* (1915) and *Women in Love* (1920) on similar lines. Infact, these two novels represent the progressive fructification of the quint-essential Lawrence genius that opens out in *Sons and Lovers*.

When I studied *Sons and Lovers* and quite some criticism on Lawrence some thirty years ago in 1962, a feeling had gripped me that many of the well-known critics on Lawrence had either not cared to comprehend his genius or deliberately misrepresented his basic concepts and technique. Subsequent perusal of Lawrence's extra-fictional writings including his *Letters*, the two volumes of *Phoenix*, *Apocalypse* and *Fantasia of the Unconscious* confirmed my initial impression. It was further confirmed by Lawrence's very recent evaluation by Martin Green. According to him "Lawrence was the one writer who, like Donne and Shelley among poets, George Eliot and Hardy among novelists suffered the most at the hands of both the specialist critic and the general reader" (Martin Green, *English Novel in the Twentieth Century*. London : Routledge and Kegan Paul, 1985, p. 48). The M.D. University gave me some annual grant and an urgent opportunity thereof pursue a short-term project and hence this study on Lawrence, however belated.

In 1991, the sixty-second anniversary of Lawrence's death, critical views are still in flux. Qualitatively, opinions are sharply divided regarding the nature and effect of Lawrence's genius. In the first category, among others, there are critics such as A.J. Selizman, Richard Aldington and Rebecca West who did not find any universal appeal in the novels of Lawrence. Anthony West held fast to the belief that it is "a mistake to treat Lawrence as a literary man" (D.H. Lawrence, *The Novelist Series*. London : Arthur Barker, 1957, p. 73). T.S. Eliot regarded Lawrence as "ignorant and untrained, snobbish and humourless...given to distinct sexual morbidity and extreme individualism" (T.S. Eliot, *After Strange Gods*. London : Faber and Faber, 1951, p. 82). In the same way, Eugene Goodheart found Lawrence simply holding "magical beliefs in an age of science" (*The Utopian Vision of D.H. Lawrence*, Chicago : Chicago Univ. Press, 1963, p. 105). Among Others who did injustice to Lawrence include W.Y. Tindall, Harry T. Moore, Elisco vivas and W.W. Robson. In the Preface to his book titled *D.H. Lawrence and Susan His Cow* Tindall points out that "the critic's first duty to a genius is to try to understand his meaning" (W.Y. Tindall, New York. Columbia Univ. Press, 1939, p. 21). Regretably, however, his book is a long exercise in his failure to understand Lawrence's meaning. Moreover, Tindall confuses the reader on every issue. Moore denounced Lawrence for being "not always objective or impersonal enough an artist" (Harry T. Moore, *The Intelligent Heart*. Landon : Heinemann, 1955, p. 71).

On the other hand there is a chain of discerning critics who have presented Lawrence in a balanced manner and in the context he had put across his ideas and in the mould in which he had cast his art. In broad terms, Moore sums up the freshly discovered folds in the dimensions of Lawrence's vision : "In the wonder of his writing an increasing number of readers are finding......that Lawrence is one of the richest reading experiences of our time" (Harry T. Moore, *The Life and Work of D.H. Lawrence*. London : Unwin Books, 1963, p. 247). Stephen Spender judged that Lawrence's "writing was a constant search for a new life" (*The Destructive Element : A Study of Modern Writers and Beliefs*. London : Jonathan Cape, 1935, p. 182). Widmer goes deeper to affirm that "Lawrence sought to transform existence" (Kingsley Widmer, *The*

Art of Perversity. Seattle : Univ. of Washington Press, 1962, p. 23). Later critics such as F.R. Leavis, a Chastened Harry T. Moore and Mark Spilka explained and analysed the fundamental features of Lawrence's novels and tried to give his long-denied place as probably the most original novelist England has produced in the twentieth Century. Leavis placed him in the Great Tradition of the English novelists and analysed thoroughly to show how he was "one of the very greatest" (F.R. Leavis, *The Great Tradition*. London : Chatto and Windus, 1945, p. 82). In the same way E.M. Forster praised Lawrence as the greatest imaginative and "the only prophetic novelist" (*Aspects of the Novel*. London : Penguin, 1964, p. 146) of our generation. It is in this broad comprehensive context that the words of Ford Madox Hueffer (1873—1939) about Lawrence : "You have got genius" ("Autobiographical Sketches", *Assorted Articles*, 1928—29. Landon : Martin Secker, 1930, p. 71) have assumed meaning.

Although Lawrence has been given his place with the important modern novelists such as Joyce, Proust and Fanlkner yet the basic concepts and the fundamental technique involved in his writings need a more straight and clearer presentation. As such, such of the cardinal aspects of his writings as the dimensions of his visions, inter-personal relationships, oedipus complex, the element of conflict, structure, the autobiographical element, and the art of characterisation need further discussion and analysis for correct appreciation. The present study constitutes one such attempt in the above contexts through exemplification from *Sons and Lovers*. Let it, however, be hoped that the future may be in a better position to interpret Lawrence's visualisations in still deeper contexts.

The completion of this project serves toward fulfilling my obligation to the M.D. University that gave me some grant to complete it. Arogya Mandir Gorakhpur (U.P.) has its own significant contribution to the speedy completion of the writing part of the project. The calm and conducive atmosphere at this pre nice home of Nature—Cure, the care and kindness of its director Dr. Vitthal Dass and his co-operative team of doctors and employees so enthused me to write-these odd 150 pages within a period of two moths. I must acknowledge my gratitude to the Librarian and the staff of M.D. University, Rohtak and the British Council Library, Delhi for their keen coopercition in supplying the material all through the progress of the project. I am so thankful to my son Surender Singh for helping the manuscript final shape and in its expeditious publication.

Rohtak
31 December, 1991

D.S. Dalal

1

Lawrence's Vision

(A) PRELIMINARY

How is one to approach Lawrence ? This looks to be a simple and straight question but difficult to answer. There can certainly be more than one legitimate and fruitful approach to any great writer. However, in case of Lawrence it is not easy to decide upon even a single approach much less a universal one to his genius. Difficulty in this regard arises mostly due to the attitude of the early critics including Rebeca West, Richard Aldington, H.J. Selizman and Stephen Potter. Studies by these critics and, infact, by all others preceding F. R. Leavis (*The Great Tradition*, 1945) and David Daiches (*The Novel and the Modern World*, 1960) are merely commentaries on the most easily applicable or explicable perspectives of Lawrence's writings. Thus, owing to the absence of sustained attempts at any comprehensive probing into the basic genius of Lawrence the entire lot of studies prior to that of F. R. Leavis presents only a muddle.

Consequent on this situation there came a number of discerning critics. These include H. M. Daleski, Horace Gregory, Harry T. Moore, John Alcorn and William Taverton. They confronted themselves with a hoard of inter-related questions with a central burden — — how is it that we go on reading certain writers century after century — — say, for example Shakespeare and Aristotle. The pursuit of such questions led them to see Lawrence as a gifted writer. They studied Lawrence's non-fiction writings such as *Letters*, *Phoenix*, *Fantasia of the Unconscious* and *Apocalypse*. These studies further revealed that in Lawrence, fiction and doctrine, technical aesthetics and prophetic vision go together. In this context the views of Lawrence can be seen and studied with advantage. In his well-known essay, "Surgery for the — the Novel — — or a Bomb". Lawrence evinced his sincere intention to bring philosophy and novel together :

> "It seems to me it was the greatest pity in the world, when philosophy and fiction got split. The two should come together again — — in the novel".[1]

In view of this discovery about the genius of Lawrence these critics formed the view that it is only after analysing his innovations, assessing his cardinal ideas and balancing his ideational meaning that the constituents of his philosophy can be comprehended. Deductively, the major tenets of Lawrentian philosophy constitute an inter-related trio. The first of these is rooted in (1) the Element of Duality, the other which, at once resolves the tangle of the first perspective and suggests a deeper and a higher comprehension of colloidal relations implies (2) Apotheosis of Sex, and the third involves the basic life principle (3) the Gospel of Blood Intimacy.

(B) MAIN FEATURES

(1) THE ELEMENT OF DUALITY

The first constituent of Lawrentian philosophy pertains to the element of universal duality in all things in the world. Very much like his personality Lawrence's art is compounded of two waves which he depicts through the relotionship between the Male and the Female — — the two poles of creation. Lawrence's central activity as a novelist was to know and show as to what was there in human personality that obstructed unity, happiness and progress. In this context Lawrence came to depict that an eternal conflict continually goes on (i) within the individual and (ii) in the world around, that is between individual and individual. And that is why Lawrence pointed out that romantic love, emotional friendship, various forms of marriage and the traditional concepts of good and virtue always stunted and dwarfed human personality.

All put together, the element of dualism is the central feature of thought and vision in Lawrence. Lawrence has sought to establish this concept both through personal proclamation and by giving a general example from nature. In any case, dualism is a universal phenomenon :

> "I know I am compounded of two waves . . . . I am framed in the struggle and embrace of two opposite waves of darkness and of light".[2]

Lawrence asserted this point further with a view to universalise. Everything that exists, even a stone, has two sides to its nature".[3] Lawrence notices that the element of duality in the larger movement of history is the same thing as the "law of life".[4] He also maintains that christianity itself is dual.

On the basis of the knowledge relevant to the above discussion Lawrence explains the element of duality as an in-built aspect of the Cosmic Order and as the external complement of the very life force. Lawrence explains the first part of this universal phenomenon in his article, "The Crown":

> As the crown represents, not victory for either, but the life — engendering struggle between Lion and Unicorn, the eagle and the dove, the tiger and the Lamb, the flesh and the spirit, the Dark and the Light".[5]

And from this analysis Lawrence deduces, as later Daleski confirms, that the resolution of conflict lies in the external balance between the conflicting forces. According to Lawrence this eternal balance above can bring about "a double reconciliation of opposites".[6] In this way, Lawrence traces the dialectics between Law and Love, Male and Female, and evinces his conviction that the conflict will never be resolved by the merger of the two forces into one or by the annihilation of one of them. On the other hand resolution lies in an effective balance between the two when they operate as pure spark. In this way, what is important and what is continually "insisted on is both the fact of opposition and the necessity for its existence".[7]

Evidently, Lawrence constructs the world on the model of male-female duality. However, the male-female opposition is not merely an instance of a dual reality but its underlying principle. In the estimate of Hough "the Male-Female opposition is an instance of dual reality but only an instance ; and Lawrence is not constructing the world on the model of sexual duality. The Father, for example, is on the same side as the female".[8] This instance is an indication of the Lawrentian conviction that "in the tension of opposites all things have their being".[9]

Illustration

A close look at *Sons and Lovers* (1913) shows that it is replete with instances of the Lawrentian concept of duality. Duality lies at the very root of the central issue of the novel. The central issue emanates from the unhealthy rather destruetive relationship between Mrs. Morel and her husband Walter Morel. Mrs. Morel evinces duality a at least two levels — — first when she wrongly evaluates the importance of her personality and role as a wife and secondly in conceiving her mission in life as a social being. She cherished the mission to culture her family but in practice confused culture with civilisation. In the first instance Gertrude made sincere and persistent efforts to reform Walter but she went only half way :

> "The pity was, she was too mueh his opposite. She could not be content with the little he might be ; she would have him the much that he ought to be. So, in seeking to make him nobler than he could be, she destroyed him".[10]

Mrs. Morel is going to have her third baby within eight years of her marriage. See the element of duality in her when she loves the children but felt wretched with the coming child. Another instance of duality can be illustrated through her peculiar attitudes. She was tired of her husband, so despised him"[11] but was at the same time "tied to him".[12] For instance, when Paul won some prize in an exhibition Mrs. Morel insisted on his telling his father : "You ought to tell your father".[13] All through the novel Mrs. Morel does two thimgs all atonce. She hates Walter but loves the children given her by him. She does so in an endeavour to realise her intense ambition through her sons but ironically enough she fails at her game through her overbearing duality :

> "Now she had two sons in the world . . . and . . . that she had put a man into each of them, that these men would work out what she wanted".[14]

This sense of pride and cherishing of ambition through the sons is quite understandable. However the duality comes to the fore when she asserts her own standards unflinchingly first in case of the husband, and now in case of the two sons — — William and Paul. William is not allowed to go on with Gyp, his fiancee. In regard to Paul she proved one too many for Miriam on all occasions, and Clara always went in some awe of her.

There was almost an extreme form of duality in Miriam. She "almost fiercely wished she were a man and yet she hated men at the same time."[15] Miriam is a dreamy impractical girl. Without realising the otherness of the other Miriam wants to possess Paul completely from the spiritual point of view, though to the total neglect of the physical. The relationship between Paul and Miriam fails vastly because she wanted to absorb Paul to fill herself up with love——love all spiritual and entirily devoid of physicality. Mrs Morel has rightly summed up Miriam's personality. She was "one of those who will want to suck a man's soul out till he has none of his own left"[16]. Thus, out of her inherent duality Miriam was selfish to the extreme. She wanted to "draw all of Paul into her."[17] Miriam revolts at the thought of human physical intimacy yet she wants to marry. To give another example, she appears to enjoy but in a self-smothering way, being in a position where she is likely to suffer. The duality in Paul lies in the phenomenon that very much like Lawrence, he lives intensely. He has immense capacity for tenderness, yet this trait of his character is sharphy balanced against his urgencies to hurt and be hurt. For instance, he hurts Miriam out of the frustration she breeds in him, and he hurts clara by the withholding of himself, his real self, in their most intimate moments.

Clara too, like Miriam, can be easily seen as a child of duality. The only difference between the two is that the first is governed by spirituality and the second by physicality. Interestingly, clara appears to be contemptuous of men but then she is mostly gripped by what we call the physical self. The essential duality in clara is summed up in the words :

> "There was a sense of mystery about her. She was so reserved, he felt she had much to reserve. Her history was open on the surface, but its inner meaning was hidden from everybody."[18]

Another level of duality in clara's nature is revealed through her relationship with Paul Morel. Her relationship with Paul chiefly lies in her strong sexuality but then she feels guilty about leaving her husband.

It is in this total context that Lawrence talks of double reconciliation of opposites. The reason is that the man and the woman are required not only to meet as opposites but to reconcile the opposing qualities within themselves. This reconciliation implies a balance and Lawrence gives religious sanctity to this transcendence of duality. He sums up his ideas thus :

> If it is to be life then it is fifty per cent me, fifty per cent thee : and the third thing, the spark, which springs from out of the balance, is timeless...Between

> man and woman, fifty per cent man and fifty per cent woman : then the pure spark. Either this, or less than nothing."[19]

(2) APOTHEOSIS OF SEX

Another of Lawrence's ceaseless endeavours was to re-orient rather revolutionise the traditional taboos regarding male-female relations. Ever since Lawrence started outlining a scheme for human redemption through effective temporal relations he could never reconcile to the notion of any barrier between brain and blood, mind and body. And so, he urged mankind "to think sexfully, honestly and completely."[20]. For him (colloidal) love and (physical) 'labour' were the fundamental essentials of life since these led to fulfilment. For this reason Lawrence emphasized that neither form of fulfilment was exclusive of the other. Unlike many, Lawrence was wary of dry intellectuality. In fact, mere cerebral Knowledge was worthless to him. It was Lawrence's conviction that "life and action originate from the great centres of dynamic consciousness,"[21] and therefore highlighted that man knows not only with the mind but also with the hoast of ganglia and the solar plexus. And knowledge thus secured was for Lawrence the real knowledge. As such, his trust in instincts and impulses accounts for his glorification of the primitive culture.

In this way, Lawrence gave unique treatment to colloidal activities in pursuance of his conviction that (*i*) sex is a primary fact of life and an underiable reality and that (*ii*) it is the very source, and the pure central fire of life. He put across these ideas so that people could understand the reality. Through this exercise he only wanted people to be truthful and never wanted to shock them. However, very few realised the sanctity of his intentions. Lawrence came to be misunderstood and became the target of critical missiles. Many like stephen Potter maligned him as an indecent person and an irresponsible writer. Certain others labelled him as a sensualist and a pornographer. This form of sharp reaction came chiefly because the element of sexual passion in novel, during the nineteenth Century, tended to disappear underground with occasional eruptious as in Emily Bronte's *Wnthering Heights* and Charlotte's *Jane Eyre*. In such cases also it was muted and obscured by imagery and irony. On the other hand, Lawrence sought to bring the entire subject in the open.

In the face of all this misunderstanding and adverse criticism it is important to note that Lawrence's treatment of sex is uninhibited and never brutal. Those who understood Lawrence in the right perspective hailed him as a liberator. For example, P.J. shepherd evaluated him as one who changed the face of the English novel by way of putting the loins into literature."[22] In point of fact, Lawrence treated the phenomenon of sex with holy reverence that needed no unnatural concealment about it. Still further, Lawrence elevates the element of sex to the level of mysticism and spirituality. For this reason he condemns Sigmund Freud and other psychoanalysts who treat sex as the basis of all human activity. He has clarified and explained the damaging effect of animality in matters of sex :

> "When man loses his deep sense of purposive, creative activity he feels lost and is lost. When he makes the sexual consummation, even in his secret soul, he falls into the beginnings of despair .....with sex as the one accepted prime motive, the world drifts into despair and anarchy."[23].

This explanation clearly shows that sex, as understood by Lawrence, is much above gross animality and his writings are a living example in this regard. Still further, he sees no difference between sex and beauty. In his well-known book, *Sex, Literature and censorship*, Lawrence equates the concept of sex with the idea of beauty :

> "Sex and beauty are inseparable, like life and consciossness. And the

> intelligence which goes with sex and beauty, and rises out of sex and beauty is intuition."[24]

Illustration

Lawrence's apotheosis of love or his preference for primitive culture of colloidal love as a source of fulfilment finds depiction in *Sons aad Lovers*. This aspect has been presented through such of the characters as Gertrude Morel, Walter Paul, Miriam and Clara.

Mrs. Gertrude Morel thinks sexfully in a vast measure but not always honestly and hence the tragedy in her life. She chose walter for her husband mainly because he appealed to her instinctivity. Soon there occurred maladiustment because neither she nor Walter realised the otherness of the other. Mrs. Morel had the best of sex relations with her husband but doubted his good intentions. After the birth of Paul she thought "What did he care about the child or her ?"[25] Then, she liked the iron constitution of her husband and wanted Paul to grow like his father. The importance of healthy sex comes to the fore as we find that after Paul developed a liking for Clara, a separated woman, she "prayed and prayed for him, that he might not be wasted."[26] In this regard, Green has called Lawrence "a prophet of eroticism"[27]. But in saying this Green seems to have lost sight of Lawrence's thrust that growth through scxual adjustment takes place within culture but which is resistent to civilization. In essential terms, Mrs Morel wrecked her happiness because of excessive use of intellect. She could never realise that a healthy, harmonious life was a pre-condition for wholeness and happiness.

At moments, Lawrence showed the importance of sex through reversal and the in—built irony. Mirian is disgusted by, and recoils from, the fact of birth as a result of animal mating, She is revolted at the thought of human physical intimacy. This is largely because her mother has made a confidente of her and given her a disproportionate view of man—women relationship. Even on an ordinary everyday level she is physically afraid as she shows in the incident when she and Paul were at the swing. The failure of Miriam's relations wtih Paul and the consequent misery is highlighted through the un-healthy and tragic thoughts of Miriam. She imagined that she could be mistress of Paul if he was so ill and weak that she could become stronger than him :

> "Then she could love him, take care of him...have him in her arms'"[28]

[Miriam did not look like a free soul. In the silent atmosphere of her home she looked liked "a maiden in bondage, her spirit dreaming in a land far away and magical."[29]

In contrast, the relationship between Miriam and Paul has been shown as a failure due to lack of understanding of the essence of sex. For instance, the intimacy between them was abstract, more a matter of soul and very little of body. Paul saw it only as a "Platonic friendship."[30] Lack of proper sex understanding nullified relationship. This basic attitude of Miriam is further shown through her fascination for flowers more than for men. At the sight of flowers Mirian felt that they were a part of her :

> "When she bent and breathed a flower, it was as if she and the flowers were loving each other. Paul hated her for it."[31]

Though Miriam sat at Paul's feet like a devotee,'[32] yet, in contrast, he liked Clara better since she had "a sort of fierceness in her."[33] In as much as such Miriam lacked physical sex, Paul's "kisses were wrong for her."[34] Sensing her mood of annoyance and disfavour, Paul told her fraukly : "You make me so spiritual ! And I don't want to be spiritual."[35] Still further, the vital importance of sex is shown through the Keenness of Miriam in a state of rivalry and prejudice. Beat rice has combed back the thick (tuft) of hair from the forehead of Paul. She wished to steal march over Beatrice : "why might she not press his body with her two hands ?"[36]

However, Miriam does not go beyond super ficialities of this sort.

As to Paul "Sex had become so complicated in him that he would have denied that he ever could want Clera or Miriam or any women whom he knew. Sex desire was a sort of detached thing, that did not belong to a woman.[37]" Paul gets definite clue about Miriam"[15] deep urge for sex. Clara informs: "She doesn't want any of your soul communion. That's your own imagination. She wants you."[38] She also added that Paul did not know it because he had never tried. In the eleventh chapter of *Sons and Lovers* titled. "The test on Miriam", Paul told himself that the root of the trouble was sort of over strong virginity in her [Miriam] and him which neither could break through.[39]" Paul was almost unaware of Miriam "as a person. She was only to him then a woman."[40] Gradually, Paul ceased to ask Miriam "to have him. Instead of drawing them together, this put them apart."[41] This terminated the already frail relationship between the two.

If Miriam is entirely intellect and spirituality then Clara is all body and passion. Her relationship with Paul is entirely physical and so brings no lasting satisfaction to them. Clara appears to know by instinct perhaps that sex is a primary fact of life and the source of pure central fire in human affairs but she did not realise the importance of spirituality. So, in her case there occurs a union of bodies but not of souls. In essential terms, effective fulfilment fructifies into harmony if spirituality is consciously accepted and practised as a vital element of life. Clara's relationship with Paul ends in a fiasco because Clara is intellectually a total bankrupt and is all flesh. This phenomenon brings us to the conclusion that ultimately it is the synthesis of the flesh and the spirit, the impulse and the reason that can yield joy and happiness.

3. Concept of Blood Intimacy

The third dimension of Lawrence's vision is covered by his concept of Blood-Intimacy. Lawrence was a Naturist and the nucleus of his Naturalistic philosophy is sustained by the comprehensive element of blood-intimacy. Together with the element of blood-intimacy, the two other aspects——Duality and Apotheosis of sex constitute the basis and the essential body of Lawrence's vision. Lawrence had no patience with any form of over-intelluctualisation in life but especially in the name of advancement of science. It was his conviction that every form of interference by intellect leads to destruction of the instinctive and intuitional life of man. In his view, too much reliance on the intellect is the root cause of evil and suffering in this world. Lawrence was on the side of instincts and pleaded return to the elemental simplicities of life. So, he sought to show how reliance on impulses can save humanity from sterile waste of spirit and retrieve happiness.

As a vitalist, a naturist and an individualist Lawrence was all out to preserve the instinctive and intuitional life of man. The comprehensive picture that evolves out of such a visualisation approximates to the cosmic mystery of life. This aspect of Lawrence's vision lies in Man's rootedness in the dark mystery of life and he could never believe in any intellectualistic orientation of life since intellect squarely obstructed the essential understanding of reality. Lawrence had unflinching faith in the sensations of the Solar Plexus (the first seat of our primal consciousness) and the dictates of the host of ganglid (complen of nerves at the pit of the stomach). In his brief tract, *Apocalypse*, Lawrence has clarified how he saw the cosmic mystery in "the magnificant here and now in flesh"[42]. In point of fact, Lawrence wanted all occurrences to be corroborated by the dictates of the blood. He thought and wrote on these lines not simply because he belonged to the Erotic Movement but the essentially instinctual sexual experience looked important to him morally and philosophically significant for man kind that was in need of happiness. As a discipline, the Erotic Movement belonged to the stream of ideas that aimed at replacing (1) ascetic religions including christianity and (2) purely intellectual disciplines and (3) expanding the moral/spiritual importance attributable to sexual experience.

At the same time, it deserves mention that abstract objective reality, ideal spiritualism like that of Shelley's

Platonism, and dry scientific facts had little meaning for Lawrence. In this context, it may be pointed out that he never felt impressed by the revolutionary theory of evolution so laboriously worked out by Charles Darwin. Lawrence said it emphatically that he didn't "care about evidence" because it did not "mean anything"[43] to him. The reason for lack of faith in scientific evidence was that it did not concile with the real experience in the region of his solar plexus. In fact, Lawrence wanted all experience to be corroborated by the dictates of the blood. Lawrence strongly realised that Man's relationship with Nature and his confidence in society was on the decrease. And therefore, he wanted to reconstruct the (individual) self by reference to "the religion of love"[44] which created a sound basis for meaningful relationships. In this context, blood-intimacy serves as a sound and effective means for moving back to our real unconscious connection with the animate world of being. Lawrence's views on his concept of blood-intimacy find best expression in his oft-quoted letter of 17 June 1913 to his friend Ernest Collins :

> My great religion is a belief in the blood, and flesh, as being wiser than intellect. We can go Wrong in our minds. But what our blood feels and believes and says, is always true[45].

In this regard Lawrence negates the intervention by such extraneous factors as the rational mind and conventional morality. From the foregoing discussion it becomes evident that man can attain his wholeness through sex and so can a woman.

Here it is necessary to explain that "Lawrence did not advocate 'sheer animalism' or destruction of the mind. He felt that the intuitional and the intellectual had fallen into Imbalance on the side of the intellectual" and so "in emphasizing our need to revive the emotional values, he was trying to restore the balance".[46] Creative impulses of man and woman are the gifts of nature, and they should not be ignored. This does not mean that mere physical sex is enough. Should it be mere physical sex, it will lead us nowhere. A balance between the physical sex and the spiritual one is needed. Infact, intellect must seek a happy union with impulse. It is in this context that Lawrence's great Religon of Blood implies a belief in the life of instincts. And that way he believed the flesh to be wiser than the intellect.

In the process of the growth of human conciousness, Lawrence stipulates that Blood Intimacy is the first meaningful stage in human relationships. Relationship between man and woman at this level implies a sort of moral which is an essential part of a novelist. In his judgement :

> "The essential function of art is moral". This tends to a morality which is "a passionate, implicit morality, not didactic." It is, in fact, "a morality which changes the blood, rather than the mind changes the blood first. The mind follows later, in the wake."[47]

In this context, it is significant to note the distinction Lawrence makes between implicit passionate morality and didactic morality. Lawrence does not believe that a work of art is immoral just because the artist has any dominant idea or purpose, the immorality comes in when the artist puts his thumb in the scale to pull it down in favour of his didactic purpose.

We get more insight into this concept of Lawrence by perusing the following extract from his leiter of June 5, 1914 to Edward Garnett :

> "I don't so much care about what the woman feels——in the contrary usage of the word —— I only care about what the woman is —— as a phenomenon."[48]

A close contextual analysis of this letter reveals that Lawrence attached due importance to the mystical aspect of colloidal intimacy which folds out with blood-intimacy. Lawrence so balances the totality of reality that on the one hand he strongly condemened Freud and other psychoanalysts who made sex the basis of all human activity and on the other came to represent the transcendent view of sex. By virtue of such a position Lawrence is comparable with Soren kierkegaard who explores cosmic dilemma to know the Inscrutable just as Lawrence explores it in an effort to find some means to resolve the phenomenon of conflict in human relationships.

Illustration

In his search for happiness Lawrence grew with the conviction that physical union with the opposite sex releases passional tides of ecstasy. And these tides, in turn, open the window to the spiritual and the mystical. If this relationship does not develop harmoniously, then mere sexual union is bound to lead to destruction. At the age of twenty three Gertrude coppard, who later became Mrs walter Morel, met walter and liked him for his physical self :

> He was erect, and very smart He had wavy black hair, and a vigorous black beard .... His cheeks were ruddy....He had...a rich, ringing laugh....He was so full of colour and animation.[49]

So, the first phase of Gertrual-walter relationship begins on the strength of Walter being passionate, impulsive, virile and instinctive. Evidently, such features of man's personality constitute the life of the flesh and the element of the Blood. After marriage, "for three months she was perpefectly happy : for six months she was very happy".[50] Then, she began asserting the life of intellect, started feeling miserable and made others more miserable. Gradually her married life becomes a hell because of her sophistications. Beyond the instinctive attachment, she started using her intellect. She felt that lack of intellectuality on Walter's part "killed her efforts at a finear intimacy."[51] She tended to be calculating and practical. On knowing that walter had neither any money nor a house of his own "her manners changed towards him."[52] The gradual alienation between Mrs Morel and walter reached the climax after the birth of the third baby (Paul) :

> Her self no longer set towards him, helplessly..... After this she scarcely desired him. And standing more aloof from him, not feeling him so much part of herself, but merely part of her circumstances, she......could leave him alone.[53]

All through her relationship with Walter, Mrs Morel tries to civilize him and, in the process, wants to put down all that was instinctive within him. Her efforts to introduce rationality in her husband and her half attachment was "like autumn"[54] in Walter's life. As it goes with walter Morel, he is a creature of impulse and instinct. So, he wants to enjoy life according to the great law of nature. On the contrary, his wife does more than everything to reform him. She talks religion and philosophy to him, and in the process destroys him both as a father and a social being.

In the same way, Paul-Miriam relationship fails to reach a satisfactory emotional adjustment. The main cause behind this failure is that Miriam is too intelligent to appreciate much that is emotional. Miriam's life is much short of the wholesome mark because "learning was the only distinction to which she thought to aspire."[55] The one obsession with Miriam was that she always wanted to "learn".[56] The other formidable reason for the failure of relationship was that Miriam "on the whole......scorned the male sex"[57]. Again, Miriam is gripped by the habit of raising everything to a level of spiritual intensity. It looked Miriam was the real girl when she was enjoying the swing. At one moment Paul caught her and "down to her bowels went the hot wave."[68] However, losing herself so was rare with Miriam ; it was never her real self. In point of fact, "she was physically afraid"[59] and always brooding. It is not too far to see that despite their often spending time together neitheir Paul nor Miriam acknowledge any love :

> "He thought he was too sane for such sentimentality, and she thought herself too lofty."[60]

It is wondered by the omniscient author : "Why was there his blood battling with her ?"[61] Therefore, despite Miriam loving Paul "absorbedly"[62] she "never realized the male he was."[63] In essential terms, the real self of Miriam is characterised by the swing at Willey Farm. She has nothing physical to offer. As such, their relationship is marked by an alternation between love and hate. This phenomenon is symbolised by the swing that advances to a point and then moves backward and so on but it makes no progress.

As against the spiritualism of Miriam the roots of Paul-Clara relationship are purely physical and that is why it crashes down. Paul-clara attachment was virtually physical. Clara "loved him (Paul) for his quick, unexpected movements, like a young animal."[64] And, Paul turns away from her in disgust, just as earlier he had turned away from Miriam. The fact, however, cannot be ignored that Paul's experience with Clara serves as the training ground for a satisfying experience in life whenever the integration of flesh and spirit was to take place.

In sum, Paul-Clara relationship fails because Clara is all instinct and Paul looks at her behaviour from a rationalistic and intellectual point of view. Clara's love is only flesh-deep and she hopelessly lacks mental and spiritual depths and therefore, Panl's soul could not be kept steady. Therefore, Clara went away and settled where she belonged. Ultimately, she goes back to Baxter Dawes, her husband because he is more instinctive than Paul. Through this relationship Lawrence shows that man does not live by the mind alone. He needs to satisfy the call of his blood or flesh so as to lead a happy balanced life.

From the above discussion it becomes evident, as Lawrence observed, that a man can only view the universe in the light of a theory, and since the novel is a microcosm, it has to reflect a micro-theory, 'some theory of being and metaphysic'. Of course, this metaphysic must not obtrude and turn the novel into a tract, nor must the novelist make himself a metapnysic of self-justification, and then apply the World to this, instead of applying this to the World.

References

1. D.H. Lawrence, *Phoenix : The Posthumous Papers of D.H. Lawrence* (London : Heinemann, 1961), p. 520. (Hereafter this book will be referred to as *Phoenix*).
2. D.H. Lawrence, "The crown", *Reflections on the Death of a Porcupine and other Essays* (Philadelphia : Centaur Press, 1925), p. 241.
3. D.H. Lawrence, "Love was once a Little Boy", *Reflection*, p. 183.
4. Lawrence H. Davidson, *Movements in European History* (London : Secker, 1921), p. 306.
5. D.H. Lawrence, *Phoenix*, p. 380—81.
6. H.M. Daleski, *The Forked Flame : A Study of D.H. Lawrence* (London : Faber, 1965), p. 71.
7. D.H. Lawrence, "The crown", *Reflections*, p. 3.
8. Graham Hough, *The Dark Sun : A study of D.H. Lawrence* (London : Gerald Duckworth, 1965), p. 225. (Hereafter this book will be referred to as *the Dark Sun*).
9. D.H. Lawrence, *Phoenix*, p. 67.
10. *Sons and Lovers* (London : Penguin Books, 1981), p. 51.
11. Ibid., p. 40.
12. Ibid., p. 40.
13. Ibid., p. 102.
14. Ibid., p. 143.
15. Ibid., p. 204.
16. Ibid., p. 211.
17. Ibid., p. 247.
18. Ibid., p. 324.
19. D.H. Lawrence, "Him with His Tail in His Mouth", *Reflections*, p. 141.
20. D.H. Lawrence, *Fantasia of the unconscious and Psycho-analysis and the unconscious* (London : Heinemann, 1961), p. 91. (Hereafter this book will be referred to as *Fantasia*).
21. *Phoenix*, p. 24.

22. P.J. Shepherd, "Lawrence : An evaluation", *Essays in Criticism*, XII (1964), p. 104.
23. D.H. Lawrence, *Fantasia*, p. 75.
24. D.H. Lawrence, *Sex, Literature and Censorship* (London : Heinemann, 1955), p. 122.
25. *Sons and Lovers*, p. 68.
26. *Sons and Lovers*, p. 317.
27. Martin Green, *The English Novel in the Twentieth Century* (London : Routledge and Kegan Paul, 1984), p. 60.
28. *Sons and Lovers*, p. 192.
29. Ibid., p. 194.
30. Ibid., p. 224.
31. Ibid., p. 225.
32. Ibid., p. 239.
33. Ibid., p. 240.
34. Ibid., p. 241.
35. Ibid., p. 241.
36. Ibid.. p. 261.
37. Ibid., p. 335.
38. Ibid., p. 338.
39. Ibid., p. 339.
40. Ibid., p. 348.
41. Ibid., p. 353.
42. D.H. Lawrence, *Aprocalypse* (Florence : G. Orioli, 1931), p. 16.
43. D.H. Lawrence, *The Letters of D.H. Lawrence*, ed. Aldous Huxley (London : Heinemann, 1956), p. 78.
44. D.H. Lawrence, *Phoenix*, p. 14.
45. Harry T. Moore, (ed), *The Collected Letters of D.H. Lawrence* (London : Heinemann, 1962), p. 179.
46. Harry T. Moore, *The Life and Works of D.H. Lawrence* (London : Unwin Books, 1963), pp. 244—45.
47. D.H. Lawrence, *Studies in Classic American Literature*, p. 162.
48. R.H. Poole and P.J. Shepherd, *D.H. Lawrence : A Selection* (London : Heinemann, 1970), pp. 69-70.
49. *Sons and Lovers*, p. 43.
50. *Sons and Lovers*, p. 46.

51. Ibid., p. 46.
52. Ibid., p. 48.
53. Ibid., p. 84.
54. Ibid., p. 84.
55. Ibid., p. 192.
56. Ibid., p. 204.
57. Ibid., p. 192.
58. Ibid., p. 200.
59. *Sons and Lovers*, p. 203.
60. Ibid., p. 213.
61. Ibid., p. 340.
62. Ibid., p. 242.
63. Ibid., p. 242.
64. Ibid., p. 325.

2

Inter-Personal Relationships

PRELIMINARY

It is often alleged that in human relationships Lawrence presents sex to the extent of pornography. Among others, Ezra Pound revealed to Harriet Monroe : "Lawrence gives me no particular pleasure. He has allowed himself freedom in his treatment of sexual matters and much of that is undeniably unhealthy"[1]. However, such a notion is the child of misunderstanding. Most people feel concerned with things around and form hasty impression but Lawrence must be seen in a different hight since he is concerned with the mystery of the flame for ever flowing. In practice, this mystery means that "Lawrence brought to his novels and stories a new, vivid, awareness of the primary things in life".[2] Lawrence may look like doing many things at a time but his chief interest lies in revealing to us the changing rainbow of our relationship"[3] which means the ever changing patterns in our relationships. Beresford has summed up this situation comprehensively. According to him "what matters supremely to Lawrence is the search for reality among the souls of people and of things".[4]

In the face of the tragic dilemma of modern life involving maladjustments, suppressions, commercialisation of instincts and emotions and the consequent blurring of values, Lawrence holds the balance by crystalising situations in human relationships. As an artist with a vision, Lawrence concentrates on the root causes of human predicament and analytically unveils the tragic tangle in exploring the polarities of human existence. His solution to the otherwise intractable problem of relationships is simple. It lies in the retrieval of old relations and in the establishment of ever-expanding new ones. In this context the very valid basis of "Lawrence being thought of as a particularly important novelist is that he believed himself to be living in a time of cosmic crisis".[5] Saturated as Lawrence was in the phenomenon of Apocalypse he considered the World to be underlying a rapid decline which should issue in a renovation and the only channel to meaningfully renovate this flow is through relationships. In as much as his books are artistic creations, the art therein, to use the words of Lawrence, "displays...the living conjunction between the self and its context".[6] In the World of Lawrence the contexts are people around the individual and the individuals around the people.

The problem of inter-personal relationships is a major issue with Lawrence. He was ever rooted in the conviction that the novel may be a way of demonstrating that it is possible to live...without accepting official version of reality. For him, the acceptable version was the living interaction between man and woman. The crux of the matter in this regard relates to the concept that any effort to dominate or possess by man or woman leads to maladjustment, disintegration and suffering. And therefore meaningful relationships can be built and sustained by mutual understanding and appreciation of the otherness of the other in living human conditions.

The issue of relationships is connected, on the negative side, with the situation when we 'deny life' and opens out into the crucial question 'how can we most deeply live' on the positive side. The truth about this enigmatic situation comes to be revealed when the relation between man and his circumambient world comes into view. This revelation evidently shows that there are three compulsions in human life :

1. An individual can do nothing but live life,
2. Every person has to learn to be himself ; his real spontaneous self,
3. Each one of us is involved in multi-levelled conflicts.

In the process of (*i*) living life and (*ii*) in the process of becoming/learning to be one self, the individual has to have (*a*) adjustment/harmonious balancing between the conscious intelligence and the unconscious, even the pre-conscious prompting (area of inner conflict) as also a (*b*) natural adjustment with the outer, in harmony with the inner in such a way that he comes to feel "a changed man, be—aureoled man".[7] This process has since been verified by Mark Schorer, Seymour Betsky and Eliseo vivas in the context of discovering thematic meaning in the novels of Lawrence.

The above theoretical analysis shows that the nature of human relationships has a wave-rhythm pattern. The distinguishing mark of this pattern is comparable with 'beat and counter beat' or the mode of rhythmic returns in music. In *Sons and Lovers* the theme of relationships is depicted through the involvements of (*i*) Gertrude Morel and Walter (*ii*) Paul Morel and his mother (*iii*) Paul Morel and Miriam Leivers and (*iv*) Paul and Clara Baxter Dawes.

Illustration

Sons and Lovers is a graphic way of showing how two persons——Mrs Morel and her husband Walter——can live together and yet be as far apart as icebergs. The reason for this occurrence is that they had denied each other in life. Walter is a simple man moved by instincts but Mrs Morel is ever governed basically by her intellect. What is there about her outer texture : "A rather small woman, of delicate mould but resolute bearing"[8] is true of her inner self as a person. In all, her tragedy comes to be caused by the one fact that she asserted her own standards unflinchingly throughout. In the early stages of marriage, the passionate and virile nature of walter pleases Gertrude immensely but very soon her enthusiasm waned away. For example, after marriage, "for three months she was perfectly happy ; for six months she was very happy".[9] Thereafter, she grew rigid and critical and thus started the vicious circle of embittering the lives of others. In the process, her married life becomes a hell due to her sophisticated pretensions and intellectual urges. In this way, Mrs Morel got tired of Walter. So much so that she later "dispised him"[10]. The only chord that prolonged the bond was the interesting phenomenon that though Gertrude hated walter yet loved the children by him. In point of fact, the Gertrude-Walter relationship had actually had its process running over at least "eight years"[11] preceding the main action of the novel and by that time Mrs Morel expected her third child.

With the passage of time Gertrude began to use her intellect more than her emotions. She became calculating and downright practical. On knowing that Walter had neither money nor a house of his own her manners "changed towards him."[12] However, alienation between them climaxes after the birth of the third baby (Paul) when she could "leave him alone"[13] and then soon it "was really over between them"[14]. This is what it is but now and then it is seen that Mrs Morel does not want her sons to misbehave with their father. Once, Walter and William were about to punch each other. She intervened though Walter called her "a nasty little bitch"[15] and added that the children were like her. After the father left, William wanted to know why she did not let him punch his father. She was surprised that William wanted to beat his own father. At this, she pointed out that she "couldn't bear it" and therefore he should "never think of it"[16]. Evidently, at heart Mrs Morel is not bad but she could not pull up well with her husband because of basic incompatibility in their nature. In brief, her nature can be qualified as what we call taut. At the death of William she sent a telegram to walter which evinces the strength of her convictions, the brevity of her expressions and the tautness of her nature:

> "Wiliam died last night.
> Let father come, bring money."[17]

Just to recapitulate, Mrs Morel's relationship with Walter is marked by fortitude in adversity, practical sense in stress and tension, and fixity of purpose in the face of worst odds. Lawrence has beautifully summed up that Gertrude was a woman of "refinement" who "goes into the lower class, and has no satisfaction in her own life"[18]. Lack of satisfaction is confined not only to her but she effectively introduces it in the life of her children, who first hate and ostracise their father and then fail to adjust with others they come to have relationships. In this way, destruction is the chief note regarding Gertrude-Walter relationship : "She was too mueh his opposite" and finally in seeking to make him nobler than he could be, she destroyed him."[19] This destruction is symptomatic of the ruin of the family.

The second instance of relationships involves Paul Morel and his mother Gertrude. This relationship has in-built stages and dimensions. The first stage comprises the expectations Paul's mother had from her sons——first William and then Paul ; the role of Mrs Morel in over-seeing Paul's relationship with Miriam and Clara and then how Paul feels about his mother, and what impression she ls eager to leave eventually. Very much as in case of *The White Peacock* (1909) where the father dies of alcoholism and the son experiences a self-annihilating feeling of isolation and lostness :

> "I felt...a sense of awful littleness and loneliness...as if I were a mere fleck drifting unconsciously through the dark".[20]

This intuition recurs frequently to Paul, in *Sons and Lovers* as he interacts with his mother. Essentially, however, Paul makes efforts, may be sporadic, to integrate himself with life. As a matter of fact, the element of conflict and duality are at the root of Lawrentian writings and these situations become manifest in the relationship between Paul and his mother. She betrays this first in visualizing her role of cultural change through the sons and then in interfering with their emotional life.

After experiencing disillusionment with her husband walter, and after the death of william, Gertrude Morel seeks to realise her ambition to culture her family through her second son Paul. Mrs Morel is in a state of creative tension in as much as she aims at shaping the cultural atmosphere of her home. May be she set the mission to culture her family through her sons when the husband, she felt, had failed her but the issue of ambition and consequently of relationships gets worse confounded when it becomes known that she herself did not know culture from civilisation. Mrs Morel wants healthy things for her sons but then she also gets a bitter dose or two in the process that she wants to avoid so assiduously. For example, Paul has great capacity for tenderness but on occasions this trait comes to be balanced by his urgencies to hurt and even get hurt in the process. Mrs Morel wished and prayed that her sons should have the iron constitution of their father. In fact, she wanted Paul to glow quite like his father.

It looks certain that Paul is trapped by the peculiarity and intensity of his relationship with his mother. Paul's mother plays the role of a guide when Paul comes into contact first with the spiritual-minded Miriam Leivers and then with the body-minded Clara Dawes, a woman separated from her husband. Eventually, Mrs Morel finds both these girls unfit for Paul and so interferes. This keenness to interfere in the affairs of all the members of her family starts with her husband. And therefore, Mrs Morel's role in the love relations of her sons is a continuation of her over-doings with her husband. Just as she first troubled and then destroyed Walter "in seeking to make him nobler than he could be"[21] she played havoc in the lives of William and Paul by asserting her own standards in the choice of female companious for her sons. Before it is the turn of Paul Mrs Morel did not allow william to go with Gyp who had caught his fancy in London. In a general sense, it was extreme indiscretion on her part to have flayed Gyp. This high-handedness breeds guilt in the mind of william. This guilt leads to conflict which is almost beyond him to resolve. His relationship with his mother was such that he could neither fully accept his mother as a source of emotional fulfilment nor reject her totally as a mentor in his personal affairs. This dilemma makes will weary of the world and he gives up the ghost unexpectedly leaving his mother in the lurch.

As a matter of fact, Mrs Morel so conditions the sons that when they come into manhood, they cannot love because their mother is the strongest power in their lives. and holds them. As soon as the young men come into contact with women there is a split. First, Paul comes into contact with Miriam Leivers but his mother has extreme jealousy against her. She cannot stand the very sight of Miriam. Paul has good feelings for Miriam's percptive capabilities but she wants to possess him completely. Owing to sexual inhibitious she has nothing to give in return and so Paul does not allow her to pocket him. Eventually, the judgement of Paul's mother finds confirmation when Paul realised that "on the whole...(she) scorned the male sex."[22] At long last Paul realised that this posture of Miriam, instead of drawing them together "put them apart."[23] After the failure of this relation Paul got attracted toward another woman, Clara by name. Clara recognized sex as a primary fact of life but had no appreciation for spirituality of any kind. Since Mrs Morel was extremely conscious about the well-being of Paul she felt extremely awed to know about her separation from her husband and her primitive fierceness. Mrs Morel was all the more frightened to know that "there was a sense of mystery about her" and that the inner meaning of her history "was hidden from everybody."[24] Therefore, Paul's relationship with Clara ended in a fiasco and Paul was eventually happy to have parted company with her, and not simply because his mother so wanted. Finally, the mother dies and Paul is left at the end naked of everything, with the drift towards death. Gradually, however, he overcomes darkness and moves toward light and life.

Most of Mrs Morel's personality remains misunderstood during her active life but just before death she looked at Paul "almost wanting him to forgive her...She was only sorry for him."[25] Finally, the mother dies and Paul "is left...naked of everyting, with the drift towards death."[26] Gradually, however, he overcomes darkness and death and moves toward light and life ; "towards the city's gold phosphorescence."[27] Not that there comes about any sudden transformation in the person of Paul, but he comes to his own with the strength left in him. All put together, the relationship between Paul and his mother stands for the essential paradox of all mother-son relationships.

The very fundamental observation that *Sons and Lovers* is primarily an enquiry into human relationships is further crystalised in reference to Paul's relationship wlth Miriam Leivers. Lawrence's conviction given out in his letters and elaborated in *Fantasia* of the *Unconscious* that exaggerated and intense spiritual love from parents leads to a painfully false relation between parents and children and also that possessive love by parents thwarts healthy love between children and the women with whom they come into contact, finds illustration in Paul-Miriam relationship. As an illustration of the above observation, it can be seen, in brief however, that Paul's relationship with Miriam begins with mere friendship, develops into deep intimacy but never grows into a living, throbbing physical reality. Also, in case of Paul it is evident that in his long drawn out web of relationships with the erring father, to his mother, brothers, and sisters he feels strong affinity with Miriam. This relationship may be defined as spiritual in quality though Paul could not sustain it beyond a measure since it did not look growing into a wholesome one.

As a dreamy, impractical and romantic girl Miriam wants to have complete possession of Paul. Paul has good feelings for Miriam's qualities of perception but does not allow her to pocket him. Interestingly enough, Miriam wants the whole substance to come to her but she has virtually nothing to give in return. Knowing fully that Miriam suffers from sexual inhibitedness Paul expects physical gratification from her. In all, their relationship never goes beyond a soul-sucking experience, and lands them only in deeper conflicts. Miriam is at once a very simple and is very complex individual. She is keen to marry but revolts at the very thought of physical intimacy. At the same time Miriam "almost fiercely wished she were a man and yet she hated men at the same time".[28] The idea of the otherness of the other is beyond her and therefore she fiercely wants to possess Paul completely from the spiritual point of view to the total neglect of the physical. The views of Mrs Morel on Miriam are highly revealing. According to her Miriam is "one of those who will want to suck a man's soul out till he has none of his own left"[29]

Besides the foregoing cause, the one more reason for the failure of relationship is the instinctive jealousy Paul's mother has for Miriam. She cannot stand the very sight of Miriam and this dilemmatic situation causes emotional crisis in the life not of Miriam alone but of all the three persons involved. For instance, after her frustrating experience in connection with Paul—Miriam relationship, she could never be her former self and gradually drifted toward death ; Paul developed links with Clara to seek gratification in her physicality whereas Miriam had no way out but to sulk. Eventually, Paul decided not to marry Miriam because in marrying her "he could not have faced his mother. It seemed to him that to sacrifice himself in a marriage he did not want, would be degrading, and would undo all his life, make it a nullity."[30] Still further, after the death of his mother and fresh meetings with Miriam and Clara Paul "understood his sexual problems to derive from his close relation to his mother, and to the failure of her marriage".[31] The other cause of the failure of relationship between Paul and Miriam is attribuatable to the fact that "on the whole...(she) scorned the male sex"[32] and then seeks to raise everything to spirituality.

Lawrence uses irony to show that Miriam is disgusted by, and recoils from, the fact of birth as a result of animal mating. May be because of her training by her mother or due to inherent proclivities Miriam is physically afraid of men as she shows in the incident with Paul when they were on the swing. Strangely enough, Miriam imagined that she could love, like and marry Paul if she could become physically stronger than him :

> "Then she could love him...take care
> of him— have him in her arms".[33]

Although Paul and Miriam were moving together yet their relationship in terms of interaction was meaningful in the least :

> "Paul looked into Miriam's eyes....Her
> soul quivered. It was the communi-
> cation she wanted".[34]

At this callousness, Paul turned aside out of pain. And how should he not feel like this when "they seem as if they walk like butterflies".[35] On the other hand, Miriam also feels odd about Paul as she thinks about him :

> "He had not seemed to belong to her
> ... ; he was different then—not her
> Paul, who understood the slightest
> quiver of her innermost soul...only

when he came right back to her,
leaving his other, his lesser self, as she
thought, would she feel alive again".[36]

So, Miriam is farthest removed from all types of passions. As a religious minded person she left even her heart's affairs to God : "Lord, if it is Thy Will that I should love him, make me love him".[37] In this way, the intimacy between them contnues to be abstract ; almost a matter of the soul——not of the whole person.

Paul was in search of a harmonious relationship but in case of Miriam he "saw it only as a Platonic friendship".[38] Miriam felt a sort of aversion for too many kisses by Paul when Paul noticed annoyance on Miriam's face, and he told her without mincing words : "you make me spiritual ! And I don't want to be spiritual."[39] As such, the relation between the two remains a failure due to lack of understanding of the essence of sex.

In point of fact, Miriam "never realized the male he was."[40] It was very rare that she lost herself as an emotional girl and the relationship essentially remained that of love and hate. This basic attitude of alteration is represented by the swing. The swing serves as a symbol to reveal Miriam's nature because, like her, it advances to a point and then moves backward and so on but it never makes any progress. At the same time this relationship could not frunctify because of her excessive intellectuality. For example, learning was the only distinction to which she thought to aspire".[41]

In spite of disappointment in all the possible ways Paul drags on with Miriam. On occasions, however, he feels better by consummating his love for Miriam. All the same, Paul's constant complaints that she is too soulful and that she is frigid, alike with the death urges he frequently experiences after intercourse with her, show that he cannot heal the split in his effective life through Miriam. Julian Moynahan has pertinently pointed out that in later stages Paul "forces his agonized relation with Miriam to the final issue of sexual union and then leaves her only when he is satisfied that they are too much at emotional cross-purposes to marry".[42] Just to recapitulate, the relationship between Paul and Miriam fails because (i) both suffered from "a sort of over strong virginity",[43] and further (ii) the circumstances at home made their marriage difficult. Still further Paul (iii) "did not want to marry".[44] After all this experience Paul had become clear on the issue :

> "Marriage was for life, and because thy had become close companions, ...he did not see that it should inevitably follow they should be man and wife".[45]

Slowly but steadily Paul stopped making any demands on Miriam and this posture, in stead of drawing them together, "put them apart".[46]

Then, Paul comes into contact with Clara Dawes. Initially they dislike each other but soon feel drawn together. Right from the beginning Paul's passion for Clara was in terms of physical need but this could not continue smoothly. However, the reasons for ineffective relationship were far from Clara being a married woman, senior in age or that her husband had attacked him. The main reason, here as in case of Miriam was that Paul could not get ideal love which he had received from the intense non-sexual parent-child relationship. This feeling once again led to inner strain.

Like Miriam, Clara too is an incomplete person. If Paul's relationship with Miriam failed because she was needlessly spiritual, in case of Clara it eventually failed because she was nothing but physical. Clara's relationship with Paul can be characterised as purely physical and hence yields no meaningful satisfaction to either of them. Clara recognized sex as a primary fact of life and the source of guiding the course of human affairs. However, she had no appreciation for spirituality. Though clara is a physical sort of self yet there is a sort of mystery about her personality :

> "There was a sense of mystery about her...Her history was open on the surface, but its inner meaning was hidden from everybody."[47]

The mystery about her deepens as we come to know that her relationship with Paul is that of strong sexuality, yet she cannot overcome the guilt in leaving her husband.

As in case of the earlier relationship, so also in case of Paul-Clara interaction Mrs Morel tried to play a constructive role. The mother provides Paul with standards of normalcy and wholeness by which he could judge both Miriam and Clara. Mrs. Morel was extremely conscious about the well-being of Paul. And after Paul developed a liking for Clara, she "prayed and prayed for him, that he might not be wasted".[48] Miriam almost worshipped Paul. She sat at his feet "like a devotee"[49] yet he felt more attracted toward Clara because she possessed "a sort of fierceness in her".[50]

Paul-clara relationship crashes down because of the one-sidedness of Clara's personality. It ends in a fiasco since Clara is discovered to be all flesh but intellectually bankrupt. Clara loved Paul with the intensity of "a young animal"[51] but Paul eventually rejected her as he had done in case of Miriam. During his experience with Clara, he discovered that she was wholly motivated by instincts and had nothing to do with intellectuality. It disgusted Paul to ponder that Clara's attachment with him was not a whit beyond the flesh and she utterly lacked intellectual and spiritual profundities.

A stage comes in Paul-Clara relationship when Paul comes to have a sense of guilt in regard to his relationship with her. Paul knows that Baxter Dawes, Clara's husband will attack him if possible. One can conclude that Paul's sense of guilt over Clara makes this necessary to him, and that the physical suffering in some way compensates for the wrong he feels he has done her husband. This alone does not satisfy Paul. He visits the sick Baxter in sheffield, and is instrumental in bringing Clara and Baxter together again. On the one hand he explains to Clara how Dawes was suffering and on the other he tells Dawes that Clara is tired of him (Paul). This mediatory stance could well be put down to a genuine desire to see them reconciled. However, some could as well interpret this gesture that since Paul was unable to have a complete relationship with a woman while his mother still lives, seeks to rid himself of the encumbrance of Clara. This action is, in fact, a spurt of altruism which Paul is always likely to display in human relations.

Paul is entirely dominant in the affair with Clara, even to the point of forcing a reconciliation between Baxter and Clara before withdrawing into a nuit Blanche of grief over his mother's death. There is a good rather healthy end to Paul-Clara relationship since she "went with her husband to shaffield and Paul scarcely saw her again".[52]

In this way, Lawrence has handled the problem of inter-personal relationships in a unique manner. However, it is alleged that Paul's relationship with Miriam and Clara were not fully tried out —— these were left mid way. And so Lawrence has looked on the consequences of these relationships like "the slaughter of the foetus in the womb".[53] But the truth is farthest removed from it. These two, like the others, were the medium for the growth of Paul——through them as through many others. Secondly, Lawrence does not want to present a depressing picture ; he is for a bright prospect. And therefore he does not show that relations in the world are comparable with either the slaughter of the foetus in the womb or that things in the world, as *Sons and Lover* depicts, are as bad as Baxter Dawes sees them. This is manifest from Baxter's out-burst to a querry by Paul about his health and if he had any, caretakers around : "I know nobody nowhere".[54]

Despite clear cut crystallization of the issue of relationships certain critics have pointed out that Lawrence has offered no solution to the problem and his explanation "does nothing at all toward the solution of the problem."[55] As a solution to this effect Lawrence aptly suggests a state of 'COUNTERPOISE' and this can be possible through double reconciliation of oppo-sites between men and women. As against Barthes, Polayni has emphasized that Lawrence's "resolution look the work of an illumined mind"'[56] This fact finds verification in the pheno-menon that ultimately Paul evolves into "a free and a whole man."[57] Evidently, in presenting the rainbow of human relationships Lawrence has not taken sides ; he has presented the whole thing objectively. Lawrence feels that failing objectivity or anywhere less than this his "genius would have been destroyed."[58] In sum, Lawrence has handled the issue of relationships comprehensively. And the observation of Lascelles Abercrombie seems highly pertinent in the total context :

> "Life, for Mr Lawrence, is a coin which has both obverse and reverse ; so it is for most people, but his unusual art consists in his surprising ability to illuminate both sides simultaneously."[59]

References

1. Ezra Pound, Letter to Harriet Monroe, September, 23, 1913, p. 105
2. Graham Handley, Brodie's Notes on D.H. Lawrence's *Sons and Lovers* (London : Pan Educational, 1967), p. 9.
3. D.H. Lawrence, "Morality and the Novel", *Phoenix*, p. 532.
4. J.D. Beresford, *The Nation*, December 8, 1923, p. 28.
5. Frank Kermode, "Lawrence and the Apocalyptic Types." *D.H. Lawrence Casebook Series* (London : The Macmillan Press Ltd., 1969), p. 205.
6. D.H. Lawrence, *The Symbolic Meaning*, p. 117.
7. D.H. Lawrence, *Phoenix*, p. 530.
8. *Sons and Lovers*, p. 37.
9. Ibid., p. 46.
10. Ibid., p. 40
11. Ibid., pp. 36-37.
12. Ibid., p. 48.
13. Ibid., p. 84.
14. Ibid., p. 85.
15. Ibid., p, 98.
16. Ibid., p. 98.
17. Ibid., p. 181.
18. D.H. Lawrence, Letter of 1912 to Edward Garnett, *Collected Letters of D.H, Lawrence*, p. I05.
19. *Sons and Lovers*, p. 51.
20. D.H. Lawrence, *The White Peacock* (1909), pp. 36-37.

21. *Sons and Lovers*, p. 51.
22. Ibid., p. 192.
23. Ibid., p. 353.
24. Ibid., p. 324.
25. Ibid.,p, 441.
26. Jane T. Boulton ed; The Letters of D.H. Lawrence (Cambridge Univ. Press, 1979), p. 477.
27. *Sons and Lovers*, p. 492.
28. Ibid., p. 204.
29. Ibid., p. 211.
30. Ibid., pp. 339-40.
31. Martin Green, *The English Novel in the Twentieth Century*, p. 61.
32. *Sons and Lovers*, p. 192.
33. Ibid., p. 192.
34. Ibid., p. 210.
35. Ibid., p. 210.
36. Ibid., p. 216.
37. Ibid., p. 223.
38. Ibid.. p. 224.
39. Ibid., p. 241.
40. Ibid., p 242.
41. Ibid., p. 192.
42. Julian Moynahan, *The Deed of Life*, p 23.
43. *Sons and Lovers*, p. 339.
44. Ibid., p. 339.
45. Ibid., p. 339.
46. Ibid., p. 353.
47. Ibid., p. 324.
48. Ibid., p. 317.
49. Ibid., p. 239.
50. Ibid., p. 240
51. Ibid., p. 325.
52. Ibid., p. 481.
53. J.T. Boulton ed., *The Letters of D.H. Lawrence* (Cambridge : CUP, 1979), p. 197.
54. *Sons and Lovers*, p. 450.

55. Ronald Barthes, Critique et Verite, trans. Malcolm Bradbury (Paris : Seuil, 1966), p, 64.
56. Michael Polayni, *The Tacit Dimension* (London : Routledge and Kegan Paul, 1967), p. 64.
57. George Zyaruk. "The Collected Letters of Jessie Chambers" D.H. *Lawrence Review* (Spring-Summer 1979, p. 66.
58. Edward Nehls, *D.H. Lawrence* : *A Composite Biography* (New York . Univ. of Wisconsin Press, 1957), p. 71.
59. R.P. Draper ed., *D.H. Lawrence* : *The Critical Heritage* (London : Routledge & Kagan Paul, 1970), p. 68.

□ □ □

3

The Oedipus Complex

PRELIMINARY

It has often been alleged that in *Sons and Lovers* Lawrence has used the Freudian concept of the Oedipus complex to present the tangle of relationships between Paul Morel and his mother, and the two girls—–Miriam Leivers and Clara Dawes. Without clearly referring to the Oedipus Complex Ezra Pound has emphatically condemned Lawrence, in a letter to Harriet Monroe : "Lawrence gives me no particular pleasure. He has allowed himself freedom in his treatment of sexual matters and much that is undeniably unhealthy".[1] As against Ezra Pound, Moynahan could never agree with those who seek to find Oedipus Complex in *Sons and Lovers.* Moynahan points out that he "totally missed the point that Paul Morel was fixated." He explains further :

> "One knew boys just as responsive to their mothers as Paul was, and it seemed natural for him to feel very sorry when she died."[2]

As such, adverse opinions are the product of misnomers and false notions. As Lawrence completed this novel in 1913, Freud had published his article on the Oedipus Complex and Psychoanalysis in 1912, and it is on record that Lawrence has disapproved of the very basic approach of Freud. All the same, whatever the value and validity of Freud's much publicised insight into human behaviour and relations, Lawrence was not favourably disposed to Freud's views.

Since Lawrence himself was involved in deep emotional attachment with his mother, readers have taken the cue from that incident of personal llfe and applied that on his novel.

Referring to the unhealthy effects of mother-fixation, Lawrence has high-lighted : "when a male child is aroused to a passionate mother-love he is liable to contract tuberculosis of the lungs at some time in his life".[3] It is significant to note that this type of disease never infected Paul. So, a close analysis of the novel and proper, rather contextual analysis of critical opinions is bound to show that misunderstanding of the concepts and hasty textual interpretations are at the root of the issue.

The Oedipus Myth is of Greek origin. Oedipus was the son of king Laius of Thebes, a city state. The oracle of Delphi prophesied that king Laius would be killed by his own son and that son would marry his mother. Terribly frightened by this, Laius had his young child exposed on a mountain in the hope that it will die there. The child was, however, saved by a compassionate servant and in course of time grew to be a strong and dauntless person. Once on his way to Delphi, king Laius met Oedipus on the way. The king tried to force the youth from the path. This uncalled—for high-handedness infuriated Oedipus and he slained the king along with his four attendants. Currently, Thebes was troubled by the Sphinx and Oedipus saved the country from the frightful creature by killing it. The Thebans felt grateful and made him their king. Soon, he married the widow of the dead king Laius, little knowing that the widowed queen was his own mother. Later, the truth came to be revealed and the queen killed herself and Oedipus put out his eyes.

Illustration

It has been felt that Lawrence used this myth to interpret the son-mother attachment in *Sons and Lovers*. Among other factors, the one apparent point against this notional proposition is that in a mythical representation of this kind at least three main basic factors are involved. These include (*i*) the role of super-human powers of gods or godesses or at least of Oracles and (*ii*) ignorance about the mother-son marriage or emotional tie and (*iii*) it should lead to destruction if not to tragic waste. In case of *Sons and Lovers* neither of these three elements is anywhere near the plot. Therefore, for any clear and dependable appreciation of the novel, what needs to be done is to locate the causes behind this misunderstanding. Besides this, certain key passages need to be interpreted in their proper contexts. Finally, it may be said that at the most, the book fictionalises a case of keen possessiveness.

There are certain symptoms in the various scenes and incidents in the novel which give one the impression, however mistaken, that there was Oedipal relationship between Paul Morel and his mother. It is argued that owing to oedipal relationship with his mother Paul tends to be incurably romantic, and often chivalrous. One manifestation, on his twenty third birlhday is that he seeks to deck his mother with sprays of flowers. Out of a romantic aspect Paul constantly refers to his mother as "my little one". He seems to treat his mother as his "girl" when he takes her out in Nottingham, Lincoln, or on holiday in Mablethorpe. Still earlier, more than a similar relationship is seen in case of Mrs. Morel's eldest son William. William won first prize in a race. As he came home the prize was placed before the mother and "she took it like a queen"[4] No one stops to think that Mrs. Morel took such a keen interest even in the little affairs of her sons because she expected to materialise her mission through her sons. For example, whenever William goes out on business she is weighed down with fear because "she was afraid of her son's going the same way as his father".[5] The text of the novel corroborates this fact that Mrs. Morel almost lived by Will since "she hoped in him so much".[6]

The scenes and passages that generate doubts as to the Oedipal nature of the novel are in plenty in the text. As Paul returned home after good day's earnings, he brought her a little spray, the best he could find. She appreciated it as "Pretty" and talked "in a curious tone, of a woman accepting a love—token".[7] Again, on their visit to the Leivers Farm "the mother and son were in ecstasy together."[8] In another scene Mrs. Morel had put on a new cotton blouse and, at his mother's very sight Paul jumped up : "Oh, my stars !... What a bobby—dazzler !"[9] whereas the mother described that as very quiet. Paul had got in absorbing love with Miriam

Leivers but Mrs. Morel did not want him to be destroyed by that girl with half-baked ideas. And, therefore, to discourage Paul from being pocketed by Miriam she shows his importance by emphasizing : "I've never had a husband—not really".[10] One can go still further with instances. In his antics, Paul being "raw and irritable ..wearied his mothor very often"[11] and owing to his inter-action with improper girls Mrs. Morel "saw the sunshine going out of him, and she resented it".[12] Such references and passages can be seen right upto the close of the novel. As Paul's mother is gradually inching towards death he frequently stresses the fact that she looks like a girl. As her illness gets worse Paul's bitterness gives way to resignation but what is significant is the outer texture of the words used :

> "She was young again....She would wake up. She would lift her eyelids. She was with him still. He bent and kissed her passionately".[13]

The entire set of passages referred to above tends to show that more often than not Paul treats his mother, and not always unconsciously, as his contemporary. At the same time he was not conscious about her scornful pride regarding his raw antics yet the over-all impression tends to stay that he loved his mother like a lover. This phenomenon can, however, be explained away by analytically showing why the attachment of Mrs. Morel was so deep with her two sons, William and Paul, and by explaining the contextual meaning and significance of certain passages in the text that have contributed to the misunderstanding.

Those who seek to prove the element of the oedipus complex in *Sons and Lovers* depend on certain scenes and passages. A contextual explanation reveals that the meaning is altogether different from what has been made out by stretching simple situations.

> "Then her thoughts turned to William. Already he was getting a big boy. Already he was top of the class, and the master said he was the smartest lad in the school. She saw him a man,

> young, full of vigour, making the world glow again for her".[14]

The passage has been infused with the device of mytonymy and as such, it contains no element of the Oedipal Complex. Seen mytonymically, and in the right context, and intent of the novelist this and like passages are revelatory of Mrs. Morel's happiness. Here, the physical growth of William and his academic standing at the school coupled with his physical vigour seem to assure her with bright thoughts for future. The over-all impression about William gives her happy thoughts at the possibility that she could realise her mission to culture the family through him since her husband had failed her in that regard. Surprisingly, people even forget that at that point of time William was only "eleven years old"[15] and how could there be anything Oedipal about mother-son relationship, if at all'. Another passage which has disturbed the minds of many who are bent upon proving the Oedipus Complcx in *Sons and Lovers* is more simple in texture than any other :

> "Paul loved to sleep with his mother. ...The warmth, the security and peace of soul, the utter comfort from the touch of the other, knits the sleep, so that it takes the body and soul completely in its healing".[16]

Perhaps, nothing needs to be misconstrued when it is learnt in the context that Paul was "laid up with an attack of bronchitis".[17] It was around the time when he had received a book about birds as a prize in a competition for young children. And what is more, the following authorial comments need to be taken in the desired context :

> "Mrs Morel's intimacy with her second son was more subtle and fine, perhaps not so passionate as with the eldest"[18]

So, the simple situation is that young Paul needs the physical closeness of his mother so that he could get a more soothing sleep in his mother's bed and have a speedy recovery.

Once Paul's mother got a new white cotton blouse. They were to go out and she appeared in the inner door way rather shyly. At this Paul jumped up and went forward. He exclaimed : "Oh, my stars...what a boody—dazzler !"[19] His mother sniffed in a little haughty manner and calmly replied : "It's very quiet,"[20] though for Paul it was awfully pretty. This reference shows simply the boy's (Paul) curiosity regarding the new blouse. This also reflects Paul's mode of talking with his fond mother. In point of fact, Paul was deeply devoted to his mother. Mrs. Morel has a pair of shoes costing eight shillings a pair and Paul used to clean them for her with as much reverence as "if they had been flowers"[21]. The relationship between the mother and the son is so simple and pious. However, for unknown reasons enthusiasts forget such transparent instances which show Paul's devotion to his mother. Another catch-phrase wrongly cited to establish Oedipus Complex in *Sons Lovers* :

> "The mother and son were in
> ecstasy together."[22]

Interestingly, what they ignore is the context and context is always the cruial factor where the right meaning is sought to be comprehended. Contextually, the mother and the son had gone to meet the Leivers family at their farm. In the enjoyable company of that family and in the open, natural surroundings they felt extremely happy. That was the simple matter. And what the readers make of it ! Again, the critical mind tends to mistake the following passage relevant to mother-son interaction and hastily label it as Oedipal whereas Paul was simply trying to calm down his mother who had got ruffled as he had stayed out till very late in the night :

> "He kissed her forehead that "he
> kew so well...His hand lingered on her
> shoulder after his Kiss."[23]

Paul had stayed out till late in the company of Miriam. His mother got upset. Soon, however, he pleased her affectionately calling her a "little woman"[24] as usual.

Over-enthusiatic readers always tend to misinterpret the innocent written word. Here is a straight expression : Mrs.

Morel "was to see herself fulfilled"[25] through her son Paul. These words have been spoken in a very broad context and that is central to the theme of the novel. Mrs morel thought she had been let down by walter in culturing the family. Failing at the level of her husband she wanted to translate her mission through her sons——first William and then Paul. So, these five words, inter-alia refer to the happiness of Paul's mother at the sight of Paul since she felt : "There was so much to come out of him"[26] and her struggle had not been in vain. Also, it was in this very context further that "all his work was hers."[27]

Likewise, the words :"She flew to him, flung her arms round him for a moment"[28] are often picked out to show the element of Oedipal complex in the novel. In point of fact, these words form a dramatic depiction of Mrs Morel's action out of sheer happiness at Paul's getting first prize for his painting in an art exhibition and nothing beyond. Oeditpal element is pointed to lie in thc words which the Omniscient anthor uses to qualify Mrs Morel's mind : "Her eyes opened... ...and she looked at him (Paul) pleadingly."[29] Two things are needed here to properly appreciate the full import of this expression——one, explanation of its intended meaning in the actual context and a proper explanation of the remaining part of the passage. Contextually, it is shown that in the advanced stage of disease Mrs Morel showed more grit and maturer undurstanding. Although she was suffering immensely, in pain for much of her waning life, yet she tried to alleviate Paul's anguish by underplaying her own agony. The second, and perhaps more significant part of the passage runs as follows :

> "...almost wanting him to forgive her. ...All the time she watched him lovingly. She was only sorry for him."[30]

The context shows that before her death she wanted to shower all her affection on Paul. Through her looks the mother wanted to communicate that she wanted to do so much for the son but failed. Since she had failed in the mission she was inconsolably sorry for him.

Let us take up yet another of the so called troublesome passages :

> "She was young again....She would wake up. She would lift her eyelids. She was with him still. He bent and kissed her passionately."[31]

If we know Lawrence's vision and understand his mind as an artist, there remains no doubt that he would never introduce Oedipal element over a corpse. His concept of sex is healthy, constructive and elevating. So, it is beyond normal visualization that people should see the Oedipal situation on occasions like this ——death of a mother. As such, the passage may look anything to anyone but it can never possibly sound Oedipal to a sound mind. Another widely talked instance to which people turn for the oedipal element is contained in the words attributed to Paul, when he was left a 'Derelict' after his mother's death :

> "He wanted her to touch him, have him alongside with her."[32]

Here, Paul is recalling now that she was alive and lamenting now that she is no more. For Paul, his mother was the only force in the world that "held him up."[32] In this context the words : "He wanted to...have him along side with her" apparently mean that he wished her to call him to his dark grave——Call him to the world of the dead. This implication becomes evident as we read the novel further. Eventually, Paul rationalised constructively and refused to "give in".[34] Instead of moving towards death, Paul moved towards the city's gold phosphorescence. He resisted death and opted for life in the humming, glowing town.

From the (foregoing) discussion it becomes evident that relation of the sons and their mother is far from the oedipal. It can best be described as that of keen possessiveness on either side. This situation is well-nigh the same that Lawrence presents in reference to the background and immediate context of the term Oedipus :

> "The old son-lover was Oedipus. The name of the new one is legion".[35]

So, broadly legion includes mutual possessiveness, and has nothing to do with the Oedipus complex. It is rather a part of her well meant life-long exercise to culture her family. When her husband let her down on the cultural front she pinned her hopes first on William and then on Paul. For example, "when william was only one year old...his mother was proud of him.[36] Again, William won acclaim of his master who described him as "the smartest lad in the school" and this made "the world glow again"[37] for his mother. William shows up well for some time. Soon, however, he wears himself out in ambitions pursuits. And, in his hectic pursuits he reflected an intesity of frustration that is more his mother's than his own. An unfortunate disease eliminated William from the pursuit. Thereafter, all the good attentions of the mother were bestowed on Paul. Paul's relationship with his mother grows in stages. After losing touch with her husband Mrs Morel craved for a true and close sympathiser. She found that even as a baby Paul was trying to understand something that was pain. This naturally drew Paul very close to his mother. There were other factors besides. As a sickly and delicate child he constantly required nursing and care. The way for his later intimacy with his affectionate mother was prepared especially after the death of his elder brother William.

A close study of the text shows that Paul's childhood was laced with incidents which show his possessive love for his mother and hers for him——his sensitivity, his artistic tendencies, his withdrawn and tender nature, and that morbid tendencey (desire to die) which he was to indulge so completely after his mother's death. All through, Paul liked to help his mother in the daily chores. Even when he was a young man courting Miriam, the turning of the home-made bread was his responsibility. During his childhood and after he was so subjected to his mother's influence that even in later life he accepted her standard of judgement in every thing. He cherished the ambition fostered by his mother to get into the middle class. Paul's relationship with his mother had given him a certain effeminacy as a result of which he could never overwhelm his mother's influence on him even in matters of his emotional relationship with young girls—— Miriam and Clara. However, in regard to these girls the attitude of Paul's mother was positive. Right from her first glimpse of Miriam she had the instinctive feeling that the girl had dest-tructive tendencies. Once Paul went out of his home in the company of Miriam and his mother brooded bitterly :

> "She wants to absorb him. She wants to draw him out...till there is nothing left of him...He will never be a man on his own feet."[38]

Therefore, she was battling with the idea as to how to save Paul from ruination. For this reason she was very happy when Paul parted company with Miriam. Similarly, it was for fear of the well-being of Paul that his mother wanted him to cut off with Clara. What she feared the most in Clara was "a sense of mystery about her."[39] Paul's mother apprehended that the element of mystery in Clara might cause irreparable harm to him. Therefore she felt relieved when Clara went back to her husband where she really belonged.

References

1. Ezra Pound, Letter to Harriet Monroe Sept. 23, 1913, *Collected Letters of D.H. Lawrence*, p. 105.
2. Julian Moynahan, *The Deed of Life*, p. 13.
3. D. H. Lawrence, *Fantasia of the Unconscious* (New York : Seltzer, 1924), pp. 70-71.
4. *Sons and Lovers*, p. 91.
5. Ibid, p. 93.
6. Ibid, p. 94.
7. Ibid., p. 108.
8. Ibid., p. 170.
9. Ibid., p. 166.
10. Ibid., p. 267.
11. Ibid., p. 232.
12. Ibid., p. 232,
13. Ibid., p. 470.
14. Ibid., p. 85.

15. Ibid., p. 87.
16. Ibid., p. 107.
17. Ibid., p. 106.
18. Ibid., p. 108.
19. Ibid., p. 166.
20. Ibid., p. 166.
21. Ibid., p. 166.
22. Ibid., p. 170.
23. Ibid., p. 212.
24. Ibid., p. 212.
25. Ibid., p. 236.
26. Ibid., p. 236.
27. Ibid., p. 236.
28. Ibid., p. 311.
29. Ibid., p. 441.
30. Ibid., p. 441.
31. Ibid., p. 470.
32. Ibid., p. 492.
33. Ibid., p. 492.
34. Ibid., p. 492.
35. *The Letters of D. H. Lawrence*. Aldous Huxley (London ; Heinemann, 1932), p. 102.
36. *Sons and Lovers*, p. 50.
37. Ibid., p. 85.
38. Ibid. p. 246,
39., Ibid., p. 324.

□□□

4

The Element of Conflict

PRELIMINARY

There are numerous views and impressions regarding the element of conflict in the novels of Lawrence. However, there is no consistent study on this topic that treats it exhaustively. And hence the need, however modest, for a fresh look and exhaustive treatment. Like the issue of relationships, the problem of conflict is relevant to the modern times and it will never lose currency. Anthony West has quoted Lawrence saying that it is "the problem of today, the establishment of new relations, or the re-adjustment of the old ones, between men and Women."[1] Arnold Kettle has confirmed that "Lawrence sees human relationships essentially in terms of a confict."[2] It is Lawrence's ability to convey across this sense of conflict——which does indeed go deeper than a rational level——and which gives his finest descriptions of personal relationships their unique quality and insight. Dorothy Van Ghent evaluates the problem in a still broader context and sees the context in the light of its application in major novelists. Accordingly, Ghent Observes :

> "Novels...deal with conflicts of one kind or another drawn from life in the sense that they are representative of real problems in life."[3]

As such, conflict is dramatically revealed at a level, when in relation to human beings Lawrence shows "the living conjunction between the self and its context."[4] In the over-all context, there emerge at least four qualitative features of

Lawrence's concept of conflict. These include (1) Conflict between culture and civilisation (2) the symbolic form of conflict (3) Conflict as born out of duality and (4) Conflict as prelude to resolution.

The first major dimension of Lawrentian concept of conflict consists in the perennial conflict between culture and civilization. Fictionally, we can identify these two concepts with the two families in E.M. Forster's *Howards End* (1910), the Schlegels and the Wilcoxes, and say that Lawrence wrote for the former. However, as a prophet of Eroticism, Lawrence presented himself to some degree as the enemy of the Schlegels and of culture. For instance, as Green points out, "he spoke against love, and for desire ; but that was a dialectical development within culture, and still a resistance to civilization."[5] Essentially, he was for culture and against the artificialities of civilization. He was clear about the distinction and showed that any confusion in that regard led to suffering. The activities of Mrs Morel form a classic instance of the case in point.

Secondly, Lawrence studies conflict in the cosmically opposed forces in nature and the social organism. What is more, he sees the opposed forces symbolically, in terms of the dark and the light, the eagle and the dove, the tiger and the lamb, or the lion and the unicorn. In Lawrence, what is continually "insisted on is both the fact of opposition and the necessity for its existence"[6] to the point indeed of turning the conflict into a raison d etre. The lion and the Unicorn would both cease to be, if either of them really won in the fight (for the crown) which is their sole reason for existing. Thus, the existence of contrary forces in life is necessary to Human Existence. F.R. Leavis was the first, in this respect, to point out "the significant parallel between Lawrence's thought and that of Blake."[7]

This point of the coexistence of opposed forces is reiterated by Lawrence in his comprehensive essay on Hardy. Therein, he has abstracted some of the prominent symbolic qualities of man and woman which are shown in the following table :

Male	*Female*
1. Movement	Stability
2. Time	Eternity
3. Registers relationships	Occupied in self feeling
4. Knowledge	Feeling
5. Spirit	Flesh
6. Service of some idea	Full life in the Body
7. Self-subordination	Self-establishment
8. Utterance	Gratification in the senses
9. Public Good	Enjoyment through the senses
10. Mental clarity	Sensation
11. Consciousness	Instinct
12. Mind	Senses
13. Knowledge	Nature
14. Brain	Body
15. Light	Darkness.

These are some of the distinct attributes of the male and female entities though it is quite unlikely that psychologists would find these distinctions acceptable. However, this is not the point at issue. The classification serves as a useful index to Lawrence's thought in regard to conflict which is, in one sense, in the fundamental opposition of entities.

Thirdly, Lawrence visualises that confiict emanates from duality which is an all pervading principle of life, and the eternal complement of the very life force. Lawrence gives currency to this point by showing its operation in the larger movement of history :

> "We must never forget that mankind lives by a two-fold motive : the motive of peace and increase, and the motive of contest and martial triumph. As soon as the appetite for martial adventure and triumph in conflict is satisfied, the appetite for peace and increase manifests itself, and vice-versa. It seems a law of life."[8]

As in movements of history so also "in nearly all great novelists Lawrence has located the element of dichotomy—— a didactic purpose... directly opposite to their passional inspiration."[9] Still further, Lawrence maintains that christianity itself is dual, being both "a religion of the strong (that teaches) renunciation and love, and a religion of the weak (that teaches) down with the strong and the powerful, and let the poor be glorified."[10]

Finally, Lawrence sees conflict as an effective prelude to resolution of the tangles involved in inter-personal relationships. Lawrence has pertinently observed that "in the tension of opposites all things have their being."[11] This, however, does not mean that conflict finds no resolution. It does. But it cannot be defined as a 'balance' since the resolution comes about "in the form of a mystery."[12] Also, the resolution cannot be so defined because the new whole which is created by establishing a relation between the opposites is not a fusing of the two into one but a complementing of the one by the other ; and the relation itself is the only absolute.

In **Sons and Lovers**, the conflict is multidimensional. And, the central conflict in the novel is so pervasive that it conditions the struggle of most of the characters to realize themselves and in turn helps explain the baffled compromise that other characters make with the circumstances into which they were born. This phenomenon is depicted through the inter-relationships of such of the characters as Mrs Morel, Paul, Miriam Leivers and clara Dawes.

Sons and Lovers depicts, for the most part, the conflict between husband and wife, terrible in its concentration and expenditure of energy. Hobsbaum has pertinently pointed out that it is as though Mrs Morel and walter Morel, husband and wife though they are, "were born to oppose each other."[13] It came to so happen because almost from the beginning they suffered from fluid relationships and fluctuating alliances. On her own, Mrs Morel like Lawrence, was "framed in the struggle and embrace of two opposite waves of darkness and of light."[14] Broadly, the areas of conflict, in Mrs Morel, are of three distinct kinds—— (1) Out of inherent duality (2) owing to the tension between the ideal and the practical and (3) the emotional and the economic.

The persistent conflict with Mrs Morel was that she was a woman of refinement and had to go to the lower class where she could get no satisfaction. So, the conflict starts with the marriage of Gertude and walter Morel and continually deepens with the birth and growth of children. It was her mission to culture her family ; she first experimented on her husband but with no success. The reason was rooted in the very diversity of the nature and quality of the character of the husband and the wife. Walter Morel was the child of instincts and she was impelled by reason and intellect. And in this sense "She was too much his opposite" and "in seeking to make him nobler than he could be, she destroyed him."[15] Despite this apparent failure the conflict continued in her mind between idealism and reality and love and hate. After the birth of Paul she had come to regard walter merely as a part of her circumstances and "could leave him alone."[16] In point of fact, Mrs Morel was tired of her husband and "despised him" but, at the same time, felt "tied to him."[17] For example, when Paul won some prize in an exhibition she advised him : "you ought to tell your father."[18] In this way, out of a deep sense of conflict in her mind Mrs Morel always tends to handle two things at a time.

Afterwards, her conflict spreads out in other directions and she begins asserting the life of intellect. Infact, she becomes pragmatic and calculating. Her growing sophisfications made the life of others miserable. On knowing that Walter was as poor as a rat and did not have even a house of his own, her manners "changed towards him."[19] So much so that she started doubting walter's sincerity. After the birth of Paul she ruminates :

> "what did he care about the
> child or her?"[20]

On occasions Gertrude was insolent and even intolerable. One night when Walter returned in a drunken state he demanded food : "Is there nothing to eat in the house"![21] On poor response, he admonished Gertrude saying that as his wife she should wait on him. At this she called him a "clumsy, drunken fool"[22] and emphatically added that she would wait on a dog at the door first".[2'] With the passage of time certain well-marked emotional pressures became apparent. For example, the children are alienated from their father and in the process his personality degenerates gradually as he feels his exclusion. Progressively, the mother more and more completely dominates the affections, aspirations and mental habits of her sons. On the other hand, the father began to look almost a liability. Once, after heavy drinks Walter Morel continued lying in bed for two mornings and "there was a feeling of misery over all the house. The children breathed the air that was poisoned, and they felt dreary".[25] Thus, it was mainly owing to conflict in Mrs Morel's mind that the husband and wife, though living together, were as far apart as icebergs.

Mrs. Morel so conditions the sons that as they orient themselves toward biological adulthood, the old split in the family becomes manifest in a new form, as an internal schism in the characters of the sons. They cannot reconcile sexual choice with idealism their mother has inculcated. William feels attached towards Gyp but the mother could not like the girl and flayed her openly. This unimaginable treatment of the girl of his fancy created guilt in his mind which resulted in conflict. William found it impossible to resolve the conflict and the inner strain led to his death. The same motif is repeated in case of Paul Morel. Paul comes into contact with Miriam Leivers. The mother fails to like this cerebral type of girl and dissuades Paul from keeping meaningful relations with her. Apart from Mrs, Morel's instinctive jealousy against Miriam she felt certain that the girl of his fancy was far from a normal girl. The mother warned Paul that Miriam would "suck" his "soul out till he has none of his own left".[26] Eventually, he withdrew and and the relationship ended in a fiasco. Meanwhile, Paul finds another girl named Clara Dawes. Mrs. Morel had no doubts that there was a mystery about Clara and began to fear the son's future. Out of anxiousness she "prayed and prayed for him, that he might not be wasted".[27] the mother was the stronger influence, Paul felt convinced and he parted ways with Miriam.

Paul Morel, like any other major character in *Sons and Lovers*, is in the clutches of conflict. Like Lawrence himself, he lives intensely. Paul's conflict mainly oscillates between (1) attachment and withdrawal (2) sense of insecurity and disillusionment besides (3) the dilemma as to whom to accept and whom to reject. There are certain crises in Paul's life and at each of these his health breaks. The first is the sudden death of his elder brother, William. Paul feels rejected or at least neglected by the only person he cares for and he gets pneumonia in consequence. This dangerous illness troubled Paul immensely but, the disease with all its pains, gave him an opportunity to re-establish closeness with his mother. Infact, from now on the obsessive quality of their mutual attachment and need becomes more apparent. Throughout Paul's relationship with Miriam, the shadow of his mother casts itself over his actions and reaction and adds to the intensity of his conflict.

In point of fact, the novel dramatizes the conflict in case of Paul between normal desires and unconscious fixations. It presents his ambivalence — — his oscillations between love and hate in the affair with Miriam and then with Clara. The novel also dramatizes the mechanism of projection whereby Paul transfers his internal conflicts to the outside world. Though he believes in the welfare of all including himself and for that matter has a rich store of tenderness yet, owing to deep-seated conflict, this aspect of his character is sharply balanced against his complusions, perhaps to hurt and get hurt. Broadly, he loves Miriam yet he hurts her out of the frustration she generates in him. In the same way, Paul hurts Clara by withholding his real self even in the most intense moments. Probably he comes to realise that he has hurt his mother too. Therefore, the mother's dislike for Miriam, ill-conceived or otherwise, together with his own physical frustration because of Miriam's physical inadequacy drive Paul to his mother. It is obvious to Paul that his mother is ill because she feels ineffective in separating Paul and Miriam, and therefore he bids good bye to her so that his mother is no longer hurt further.

Conflict takes another turn consequent on the death of Paul's mother. After his mother's death, Paul returns to Miriam perhaps seeking marriage as the basis of social security. But more than that, and significantly, he goes to Miriam to make a fresh endeavour to assess and understand whether she was a fit girl for him as his wife. After his mother's death Paul becomes unhinged. He lives in a delirium of the spirit :

> "Always alone, his soul oscillated
> . . . . It made him pant".[28]

It becomes clear that when his mother withdraws her love for him, Paul becomes physically ill, and when she dies he becomes scarred. His own life, in both instances, is in the balance. In the final scene of the book, it seems Paul finds answer to his dilemma. At the time of his mother's death he voluntarily gives up Clara, knowing that there is but one direction he can take, and that is to go with his mother. At the end Paul is left emotionally derelict, with only the "drift toward death". Conflict goes on even at this level, he faces dark realities but finally he does see a bright ray and survives the gloom and depression. In this way, escapes the otherwise inexorable clutches of conflict. And finally. when almost all his conflicts are resolved, Paul Morel evolves into "a free and a whole man".[29]

Miriam Leivers represents a complex case of multiple conflicts in her relationships because there is an extreme form of duality in her. To give a self-speaking instance, Miriam "almost fiercely wished she were a man and yet she hated men at the same time".[30] As a practical manifestation of this trait she wants to possess Paul wholly from the spiritual point of view but to the total neglect of the physical aspect. Owing to her inherent conflict she always behaves in an extremely selfish manner. She craves to "draw all of Paul into her",[31] but without bothering to realise that the whole of Paul also implies an equally important physical side. Similarly, she virtually revolts at the thought of human physical intimacy yet she wants to marry. Miriam's deep internal conflict comes to the fore as she is said to enjoy things though in a self-smothering manner and can always retain the position where she is likely to suffer.

Surprisingly, Miriam imagines that she may become the mistress of Paul only if he becomes so ill and weak that she looks stronger :

> "Then she could love him
> . . . have him in her arms".[32]

In all, her thoughts are far from practical and so, "her spirit dreaming in a land far away and magical".[33] As such, owing to her in-built conflict she could never understand the essence of life. She is so spiritual-minded that even Paul's "kisses were wrong for her"[34] and she did not have the mental clarity to understand Paul's mind as he tells her frankly that he does not "want to be spiritual".[35] Conflict never allows Miriam to grow into a wholesome person or to have healthy, normal relationship with others. Her one troublesome complex is that she always wants to "learn"[36] and aspires to secure distinction in learning dry things other than real life. That is why, for all the long company of each other, neither of them acknowledges any love ;

> "He thought he was too sane for such sentimentality, and she thought herself too lofty".[37]

As such, Miriam's life is easily comparable with the Swing that oscillates but never makes any progress or advancement.

Like Miriam, Clara too, suffers from conflict, though of a different and very straight nature. Initially, Paul and Clara dislike each other but soon feel drawn together. Both these persons have conflict peculiar to them and want its resolution through each other. This becomes impossible because both are inadequate in their respective spheres. Paul's passion for Clara is only physical and so unwholesome and, therefore, their relationship fails to continue smoothly. Paul does not get wholesome love since Clara does not understand the essence of sex. This feeling naturally leads to inner strain ; the conflict continues and they part company. Interstingly Clara has contempt for most men but at the same time she is mostly gripped by what may be defined as physicality. Mrs. Morel's words about Clara seem to be thoroughly pertinent :

> "There was a sense of mystery about her .... Her history was open on the surface, but its inner meaning was hidden from everybody,'.[38]

In as much as Clara is a mysterious person, her conflict is such that between her and Paul there occurs a union of bodies but never that of souls.

Yet another instance of Clara's conflict is perceptible in the fascinating phenomenon that she is attracted to Paul on grounds of sexuality. She loves him with the intensity of "a young animal"[39] but never succeeds in overcoming the sense of guilt about deserting her husband. In this regard Clara falls much short of the spirit of Lawrence's dictum : "Think sex-fully, honestly and completely"[40] and hence the conflict and the suffering. Clara's love for Paul is only flesh-deep and so, she fails to keep his soul steady. She is nothing beyond instinct and he judges her from the intellectual point of view and therefore the relationship crashes down.

In the later phase Paul develops a sense of guilt over his relationship with her. He apprehends that Clara's husband will attack him and also feels that the impending physical suffering will compensate for the wrong he has done Baxter. With these ideas in mind, and in a bid to resolve the conflict Paul visits Baxter in the hospital and finally succeeds in bringing them together. With this success Paul vastly resolves at least one level of his life-long chain of conflicts.

Yet another point of discussion in regard to Lawrence's concept of conflict is that of its resolution. In nearly everything Lawrence wrote, he found that a phoenix-like rebirth had a suitable image for any meaningful change. Lawrence was imbued with a view of the world in which man, as he had thus far developed, was less than human, and in which "man, like the phoenix, would have to die before he could be reborn from his own ashes".[41] This point finds corroboration and exemplification through different characters in *Sons and Lovers* (1913), *The Rainbow* (1915) and finally *Women in Love* (1920). In *Women in Love* the point gets crystallized in terms of the relationship between Ursula and Birkin. With Lawrence, unbridled sexuality is far from the primary concern. It is an integrated view of sex and mutual love leading to something positive and creative. Birkin echoes this idea when he says to Ursula once :

> "What want is a strange conjunction with you not mingling and meeting ; but an equilibrium, a pure balance of two single things, as the stars balance each other".[42]

Contextually, he compares man to sea and woman to river — — each sustaining the other, complementing the other.

However. in representing the crucial process and final stage of resolution, the use of the word 'balance' should be avoided. This precaution is necessary because, solution in Lawrence is a movement from one extreme to the other of forces within the individual. However, the word that aptly suggests solution is 'counterpoise' which Lawrence believes to be nccessary in personal relations. Where the relationship is that between a man and a woman, there is a double reconciliation of opposites, for the man and the woman are required not only to meet as opposites but, as we have seen in the foregoing discussion, to reconcile the opposing qualities withing themselves. The relationship is envisaged as a meeting on equal terms of two people who have themselves achieved full individuality and transcended their duality in the balance that is attained between them :

> "If it is to be life then it is fifty percent me, fifty percent thee : and the third thing, the spark, which springs from out of the balance. is timeless . . . . Between man and woman, fifty per man and fifty per cent woman : then the pure spark. Either this, or less than nothing".[43]

Mary Freeman has aptly summed up Lawrence's position in this regard :

> "He was not willing to accept a confusion of opposites as a resolution of them. He wanted to distinguish between them, especially between the desirable and the undesirable, and yet be basically at one with some universal whole".[44]

Since the genesis of conflict lies in the fact that "everybody's behaviour is indeterminately modified by the conviction that he is living through a crisis",[45] therefore, the resolution will lie at the stage when the individual feels he has come out of the crisis.

References

1. Anthony West, *D. H. Lawrence, The Novelist Series* (London : Arthur Barker, 1951), p. 146.
2. Arnold Kettle, *An Introduction to the English Novel* (London : Hutchinson Univ. Library, 1953), p. 104.
3. Dorothy Van Ghent, "On sons and Lovers," *D. H. Lawrence : A Collection of Critical Essays* (Englewood Cliffs : Prentice Hall, 1963), p. 15.
4. D. H. Lawrence, *The Symbolic Meaning*, p. 117.
5. Martin Green, *The English Novel in the Twentieth Century* (London : Routledge & Kegan Paul, 1984), p. 60.
6. D. H. Lawrence, "The Crown", *Reflections*, p. 3.
7. F. R. Leavis, "D. H. Lawrence", *For Continuity* (Cambridge : CUP, 1933), p. 112.
8. Lawrence H. Davison (Pseud), *Movements in European History* (London, 1921), p. 306.
9. D. H. Lawrence, "The Novel", *Reflections*, p. 105.
10. D. H. Lawrence, *Twilight in Italy* (London, 1916), p. 29.
11. D. H. Lawrence, *Phoenix*, p. 67.
12. Henry Miller, "Creative Death", *The Wisdom of the Heart* (London, 1947), p. 10.
13. Philip Hobsbaum, *A Reader's Guide to D. H. Lawrence* (London : Thames and Hudson, 1981), p. 48.
14. D. H. Lawrence, "The Crown", *Reflections*, p. 241.
15. *Sons and Lovers*, p.51.
16. Ibid., p. 84.

17. Ibid., p. 40.
18. Ibid., p. 102.
19. Ibid., p. 48.
20. Ibid., p. 68.
21. Ibid., p. 75.
22. Ibid., p. 76.
23. Ibid., p. 76.
24. Ibid., p. 79.
25. Ibid., p. 79.
26. Ibid., p. 211.
27. Ibid., p. 317.
28. Ibib., p. 484.
29. George Zytaruk, "The Collected Letters of Jessie Chambers", *D. H. Lawrence Review* (Spring—Summer 1979), p. 66.
30. *Sons and Lovers*, p, 204.
31. Ibid., p. 247.
32. Ibid., p. 192.
33. Ibid., p. 194.
34. Ibid., p. 241.
35. Ibid., p. 241.
36. Ibid., p. 204.
37. Ibid., p 213.
38. Ibid., p. 324.
39. Ibid., p, 325.
40. D. H. Lawrence, *Fantasia*, p. 91.
41. Frederick R Karl, *A Reader's Guide to Great Twentieth—Century English Novels*, p. 151.
42. D. H. Lawrence, *Women in Love* ed. Charles Ross (Middlesex : Penguin Books, 1975). p. 164.
43. D. H. Lawrence, "Him with His Tail in His Mouth", *Reflections*, p. 141.
44. Mary Freeman, *D. H. Lawrence : A Basic Study of His Ideas* (Gresset & Dunlap : New York, 1955), p. 81.
45. Frank Kermode, "World in the Desert", *Critical Quarterly*, X (Spring 1968), p. 27.

□□□

5

Structure

PRELIMINARY

Lawerence has often been criticised for not living upto the critics' conception of an artist novelist. It is alleged that Lawrence's performance as an artist is uneven all through but especially in the structure of *Sons ank Lovers.* In the judgement of Harry T. Moore, the novel has "awkward moments, digressions, collapses of theme and structure."[1] According to W.W. Robson, Lawrence permits himself liberties incompatible with Flaubertian principles of art, but with the practice of any art"[2]. In the opinion of Kermode Lawrence was "a clerky writer"[3]. Again, Middleton Murry refuses to see the artist in Lawrence and asserts : "Lawrence was not, primarily, an artist ; he knew it, he declared it, his books reveal it"[4]. In his other book, *Son of Woman* (1931) Murry is even more emphatic : "Art was not his aim" (p. 234). Still further, Anthony West has observed that certain persons, including Lawrence himself, seek to justify the structure of Lawrence's novels, bad as it is, in the light of the aesthetic approach. However, he describes this approach as "something of an absurdity"[5]. West presses his point further and more emphatically : "It is a mistake to treat Lawrence as a literary man" since his novels "were not supposed to be works of art"[6]. To Hobsbaum, *Sons and Lovers* "seems vivid in parts, amorphous as a whole"[7]. It is also charged with equal vehemence that Lawrence's "novels are wayward and natural, rambling landscapes rather than cunningly constructed gardens."[8]

It is no less argued that some portions of *Sons and Lovers* are over-written ; complex people are made to act and feel in complex ways in fundamentally simple situations. Intermittently there are gaps in the widely publicised organic organisation, giving the impression of hastiness in composition. Many critics have pointed out that Lawrence's structures have suffered because he has written idea-oriented novels, and the structure gets lost in the effort to understand the novel in the context of those ideas. Above other things, it is pointed out that Lawrence himself has contributed to the corpus of confusion regarding the structure of his novels. Buter has quoted Lawrence as having said : "Novel can be created without structure."[9] However, for a proper understanding of Lawrence's mind and art, it is necessary to comprehend his words in the right context. In point of fact, he wanted to emphasize that spontaneity in art was the first principle with him and therefore, he was impatient of art "too much cooked in the artistic consciousness."[10]

One would be absurdly unrealistic to say that Lawrence's novels have neither form nor structure because a work of art can not exist without a form. What is to be significantly seen is that the form of his novel is vastly determined by the structure of the emotional experience that the text embodies. Therefore, he never much cared about the traditional modes of structure and fashioned his own rules. And, as such, in response to a communication from Arnold Bennett, he asked his literary agent to tell Bennett :

> "That all rules of construction hold good only for novels that are copies of other novels. A novel which is not a copy of other books has its own construction, and what he calls faults, he being an imitator, is what I call characteristics."[11]

[Lawrence has made a more deeply revealing observation in his letter to the Italian critic Carlo Linati :

> "Do you think that books should be sort of toys, nicely built up of observations and sensations, all finished and

> complete ? I don't....I can't bear art that you can walk round and admire. A book should be either a bandit or a rebel or a man is a coward....you need not compla in that I don't subject the intensity of my vision...or whatever it is...to some vast and imposing rhythm...I never will....Whoever reads me will be in the thick of the scrimmage, and if he wants a safe seat in the audience let him read somebody else."[12]

[Evidently, it seems pointless to blame Lawrence for not writing the kind of rounded off books one could put on the shelf and admire, which he refused to write. In point of fact, Lawrence's entire attitude in this regard was revealed as early as 1909 (even before his first novel had appeared) when he said in a letter to Blanche Jennings that "he would rather write crude living things than beautiful dead one's".[18] So, it is useless to try to discuss Lawrence's novels as "a series of discrete aesthetic organisations to be valued solely for richness of texture and internal coherence of organisation."[14]

Before resuming any detailed discussion on the structure of *Sons and Lovers*, it seems advisable to have a look at the qualitative nature of a story, a plot and the structure. A story is "a narrative of events arranged in their time-sequence. A plot is also a narrative of events, the emphasis falling on causality." For example, "the king died and then the queen died, is a story. The king died and then the queen died of grief, is a plot. The time-sequence is preserved, but the sense of causality overshadows it."[15] [In other words, a plot is an "ordered organized sequence of events and actions."[16] Structure and plot are closely related to each other but the term 'Structure' refers to something rather different from plot. "If we think of the plot as the way in which its story is arranged, its structure involves more than its story, encompassing the work's total organisation as a piece of literature, a work of art."[17] Structure involves plot, thematics, and form : it refers to our sense of a novel's over all organization and patterning, the way in which its component parts fit together to produce a totality, a satisfying whole ..or, of course, the way in which they fail so to do.

Preceding any further and deeper probe and analysis of the structure of *Sons and Lovers* (1913) it is essential to have at least a cursory view of the novel's essential plot and the vital curves in it. It tells "a simple strong simply, with none of the artistsc self-consciousness...with none of the obvious complex structure."[18] The plot of *Sons and Lovers* concerns the lives of the Morel family in a mining village in the Midlands. It opens out with the interaction of Mrs. (Gertrude) Morel and her husband Walter Morel. Mrs. Morel comes from a middle class family and goes into the lower class. After marriage her disillusionment with the economic and social status of her husband leads to frustration. She is gradually alienated from her husband and this creates an unhealthy effect on the children. The husband drinks regularly, often keeping his wife short of essential housekeeping money, and when he is drunk he is sometimes violent. Mrs. Morel brings up her family to abhor drink and despise their father.

Mrs. Morel is ambitious for her sons, and tends to live for them and her hopes of their successful future. William, the eldest, helps to realise these hopes by doing very well at school and, ultimately, getting a job wiih a shipping firm in London. Paul, the second son, discontinues schooling early, and obtains a position with Thomas Jordan, surgical appliance manufacturer, in Nottingham. Mrs. Morel seems well on the way to seeing her ambitions realised, but William becomes enamoured of a socially pretentious girl, named Gyp. The mother discourages william that his engagement with her will bring more worry than happiness. The affair ends but william gets ill and dies of pneumonia. The shadow of this death casts itself long over the family, but falls more immediately on Paul. He feels neglected because of his mother's absorption in the death of William, becomes run down and also contracts pneumonia. He is nursed by his mother and recovers.

While Paul is convalescing his mother takes him to some friends of hers, the Leivers, who live at Willey Farm. The young man becomes friendly with Miriam, a daughter of the house. His friendship with Miriam deepens into an intimate relationship but never of love. He discovers her to be highly spriritual, unpractical and possessive but she has nothing to return on the physical plane. Mrs. Morel and most of Paul's friends dislike Miriam and eventually he too comes to realise that the spiritual aspect of love by itself is not enough for him and the relationship ends. Meanwhile, Miriam introduces him to a friend of hers, Clara Dawes, a firm believer in women's rights and who is separated from her husband. After initial dislike of each other, they draw much closer together, and eventually become lovers. Around this time, Paul discovers that his mother is ill. Meanwhile, the other Morel children are settling. Annie marries her dependable Leonard and moves to Sheffield ; Arthur, in a moment of impetuosity, joins the army, but later marries Beatrice wyld, leaves the army for a steady job and succumbs to domestic life.

As Paul becomes more intimate with Clara, his mother's illness worsens. One night Paul is attacked and beaten by Baxter Dawes, Clara's husband. He recovers, nursed back to strength once again by his mother, and takes a short holiday. In the meantime, he discovers that his mother is very ill indeed. Paul gets a specialist to examine her and the disease is diagnosed as cancer. She is gradually dying and her end is hastended by Paul and Annie who give her an overdose of morphia in her milk. He has already brought Baxter and Clara together again. After his mother's death, he seeks out Mirriam, but soon realises that his future does not lie with her. His mother's death had left him a derelict. He hovers between the wish to join his mother in death and the desire to go on living. The last words of the novel——"He walked towards the faintly humming, glowing town, quickly"[19] —— perhaps reflect his determination to keep a hold on life whatever the cost.

As to the major curves in the plot of the novel, the book falls naturally and easily into the following sections :

(1) The description of the Morel family and its domestic disharmony brought about by the drinking of the father. This leads us to

(2) the focus being squarely on Mrs. Morel, William and Paul, which prepares the way for

(3) the death of William and the family reaction, with a sharper focus on Paul when he becomes seriously ill.

Part II of the book, which covers the life of Paul from the late teens to the mid-twenties, is concerned exclusively until with the him serious illness and subsequent death of Mrs. Morel. Everything is seen through Paul's eyes ; this is a contrast with the first three Chapters of Part I, in which Mrs. Morel was the acknowledged stand point from which most incidents were viewed. The divisions in Part II are as follows :

(1) Paul, in late adolescence, falls spiritually in love with Miriam Leivers. This continues for some time until he

(2) rejects Miriam because of his feeling for Clara Dawes, Miriam's friend, a believer in women's rights and who is separated from her husband.

(3) Describes the gradual ripening of Paul's physical passion for Clara, her response to it, and their coming together.

(4) Paul, beaten up by Baxter Dawes, is nursed by his mother and grows away from Clara.

(5) The illness, leading to the death of Mrs. Morel and, as an action running parallel to it Paul, realising that he cannot give himself fully to a woman while his mother lives, brings about a reconciliation between Clara and Baxter.

(6) Paul's reaction after his mother's death, his re-meeting Miriam, and his apparent will to carry on after the temptation of sucide.

Within the bare frame-work outlined above, it is worth noting that the chapter headings are clear sign posts to the road the novel is taking. Generally, each one indicates the main bias of the chapter, but inevitably material not covered by the suggestion of the title is included. The open ending gives the novel firmness, at the same time completing the naturalness which has been its main characteristic throughout. Whether it is instinct or art, the parts of the novel cohere just as the various parts of our lives cohere, and the formative flow of existence gives *Sons and Lovers* a structural unity which is never artificial or aribitrary.

Evidently, Lawrence was conscious about the form and structure of *Sons and Lovers*. And, on the strength of his consciousness he told Garnett that he "had slaved like a Turk"[20] at its structure. Lawrence wrote to Garnett, his publisher with a sense of conviction :

> "I tell you it has got form...form : haven't I made it patiently, out of sweat as well as blood ?"[21]

Despite this thoroughly pertinent classification and assertion, Edward Garnett, Lawrence's friend and publisher felt that the novel still needed extensive cutting and some shaping. Lawrence ultimately allowed him to take out what he thought necessary. And, Garnett removed about one tenth of the novel and it emerged more tight and more smooth. Lawrence was quite satisfied when he saw the proofs and wrote to Garnet :

> "You did the pruning jolly well, and I am grateful. I hope you'll live a very long time, to barber up my novels for me before they're published. I wish I were not profuse...or prolix."[22]

The position regarding the structure of *Sons and Lovers* is so clear that it has been handled on sound footing, though of a lyrical kind. But the critics do not seem to realise that all the pruning etc was necessitated in the pre-publication stage and it was a fine piece of writing after the well-meant prunings by Garnett. However, it goes without saying that discerning readers acknowledged the worth of Lawrence's genius right when the novel was released. An unsigned review in *Standard*, June 1913 highlighted that "no other English novelist of our time has so great a power to translate passion into words, but that is neither the beginning nor the end of his art."[23] Lascelles Abercrombie has expressed his views still more emphatically in his review in the *Manchester Guardian* especially regarding the str"cture of the novel under discussion :

> "The scope and variety of...his power of lighting a train of ordinary events to blaze into singular significance, make *Sons and Lovers* stand out from the fiction of the day as an achievement of the first quality."[24]

MAIN FEATURES OF STRUCTURE

All put together, the organisation of the structure of *Sons and Lovers* can be seen, for convenience of straight comprehension, in the light of a five-fold rhythmic pattern. This pattern includes such of the features of structure as

(1) Inner-Logic (2) Inter-Personal relationships
(3) The Element of conflict
(4) Structural Orientation in Scenes and characters and
(5) Symbolism.

(I) INNER LOGIC

The three main features of Lawrence's vision (A) Duality (B) Apotheosis of sex and (*c*) Blood Intimacy constitute the inner logic of the structure of *Sons and Lovers*. In Lawrentian dispensation (A) duality forms the very core of human existence as of the cosmos. Lawrence knew that even a stone has two sides to its nature,"[25] and therefore duality is the eternal complement of the very life force. Infact, Lawrence wanted to know and show as to what was there in human personality that obstructed unity, happiness and progress. Cogitations in this regard yielded the conviction that, owing to inherent duality in man, an eternal conflict goes on (I) within the individual and (2) in the world around...between individual and individual. However, this does not mean that there is no resolution of the tangle. what is needed is "not mingling and meeting ; but an equilibrium, a pure balance of two single things, as the stars balance each other."[26] Since solution in Lawrence implies a movement from one extreme to the other of forces within the individual, therefore, the apt word would be 'counterpoise' rather than balance. The element of duality is perceptible right in the central issue of *Sons and Lovers* ; it emanates from the destructive relationship between Mrs. (Gertrude) Morel and Walter, her husband. She is impelled by duality first in choosing her husband and then in conceiving her mission as a married woman. She cherishes the mission to culture her family but, in practice, gets lost in tinkering with the process of civilising her family. She destroys Walter in the misdirected effort to reform him and then ruins her sons and her self in the process. The eldest son William develops fancy for Gyp, the mother obstructs the relationship with the best of intention but this leads to acute conflict in William's mind and to his untimely demise. The second son, Paul goes close to Miriam Leivers but the mother intervenes thinking: "He is such a gaby as to let himself be absorbed. She will never let him become a man".[27] This role of Mrs. Morel causes a complex in Paul's mind as also in that of Miriam and the relationship crashes. In case of Paul Clara relationship, besides the interruption by Mrs. Morel, the inherent duality of Clara herself proves disasterous. For example, she is contemptuous of men but is perpetually gripped by physicality. Not only that Clara cannot give wholesome love to Paul, she also cannot overcome the guilt in having left her husband and the relationship ends in a fiasco.

(B) Lawrence has elevated the concept of sex to the level of mysticism and deifies it. He visualises redeeming humanity through effective temporal relations and so does not see any barrier between brain and blood, mind and body. Therefore, he urges mankind to "think sexfully, honestly and completely."[28] For Lawrence, colloidal 'love' and physical 'labour' are the essentials of life because fulfilment lies through them. As a corollary to this, Lawrence has aversion for dry intellectuality. In such matters. he has trust in instincts and impulses and glorifies primitive culture. Here, it is worth noting that Lawrence's treatment of sex is uninhibited but never brutal.

This aspect of Lawrence's vision is depicted in *Sons and Lovers* through the interplay of different characters. Mrs. Morel thinks sexfully in a vast measure but not always honestly and hence the tragedy in her life. For six months she was happy with her husband but later, especially after the birth of

Paul she begins to doubt Walters's sincerity : "What did he care about the child or her ?"[29] The short tale of Mrs Morel's long suffering starts when she begins regarding Walter as nothing more than a part of her circumstances. In case of Paul-Miriam relationship there operates a barrier between brain and blood. Miriam is over-possessive, vaguely thinks about sex, and does not know how to think honestly. She depends on intellect more than emotions. She recoils from the fact of birth as a result of animal mating. She never realises that man is both body and soul, and for a whole, complete, healthy life the body must not be denied. She never thinks sexfully and honestly and so fails to marry and secure happiness. Then, Paul shifts to Clara Dawes. No doubt, Miriam used to worship Paul "like a devotee"[30] but he likes Clara better because she has "a sort of fierceness...in her".[31] Despite this initial mutual attraction the relationship fails to fructify because Clara is an incomplete person. If Paul-Miriam relationship collapses because Miriam is all intellect, then Paul-Clara relationship comes to a naught because clara is all body and no soul.

(*c*) The third aspect, at once of Lawrence's vision and of the inner logic in the structure of *Sons and Lovers* is relevant to Lawrence's concept of Blood Intimacy. As a vitalist, Lawrence was keen to preserve the instinctive and intuitional life of man and, therefore, strongly felt that too much reliance, on intellect was the root cause of evil and suffering in human life. Lawrence has unflinching faith in the sensations of the Solar Plexus and the dictates of the host of ganglia and sees the cosmic mystery in "the magnificent here and now in flesh"[32] In his letter of 17 June 1913 to his friend Ernest Collins, Lawrence puts the point vividly :

> "My great religion is a belief in the
> blood...We can go wrong in our minds.
> But what our blood feels and believes
> and says, is always true."[33]

Here, it is necessary to clarify that Lawrence never advocates sheer animalism' or the destruction of the mind. He is rather emphatic that should it be mere physical sex, it cannot lead us anywhere. As a young women, Gertrude coppard meets Walter Morel and likes him for his ':vigorous black beard,", "ruddy" cheeks, and 'ringing laugh."[34] It is revealing that, after marriage, for three months, she was perfectly happy ; for six months, She was very happy".[35] Mrs. Morel's happiness is born out of instinctive attachment with her husband but afterwards she takes to the life of intellect and this changed attitude causes misery to all concerned. In case of Walter, this half attachment works "like autumn in (his) life".[36] Like Mrs. Morel, Miriam too is not a whole person. Though a young girl yet losing herself emotionally is never her real self; for her shimmeriness is the real thing."[37] Desire for the body is normal in a young woman but "she was physically afraid"[38] and for reason whereof Miriam "never realises the male he (Paul) was"[39]. In point of fact, "she scorned the male sex."[40] And, owing to lack of Blood (Emotional) Intimacy the relationship between Miriam and Paul failed and even then she wondered : "Why was there his blood battling with her ?[41] At the same time, Miriam relied on her intellect rather heavily. Infact, learning was the only distinction to which she thought to aspire".[42] Eventually, the relationship failed. The attraction between Paul and Clara is virtually physical. Clara "loved him (Paul) for his quick, unexpected movements, like a young animal."[43] Paul is in search of healthy love but clara is mere physicality and so fails to hold his soul steadily. After Paul is beaten by her husband she never feels the same for him since he is found physically inferior to Baxter. Consequently, her conflict, as to why did she desert her husband intensifies, and finally her mysterious nature asserts and she goes back to her husband where she really belongs.

(2) PERSONAL RELATIONSHIP

The second element of the structure of *Sons and Lovers* is relevant to the phenomenon of inter-personal relationships. This phenomenon pervades the entire book in so far as it emanates from Lawrence's vision, involved in the conflict of different characters who are, all put together, a vital part of the exercise that results in the formation of the novel's structure, That is why all the characters are engaged in "the establishment of new relations, or the re-adjuftment of the old ones."[44] stephen spender qualifies this human interaction as essentially "the tension between art and life."[49] The chain of relationships begins with Mrs. Moral and her husband. Since the issue of relationships is very cpmplex, structurally it can be best put as an angle (view-point) to see the rainbow of human interactions in the context of their mission and role in total life, their confiict, their keeness to resolve them and the consequences. In this regard, Mrs. Morel set her aim to culture her family. But. since she confuses culture with civilization, she causes disturbance in the life of all those with whom she comes into contact. As against her sophistications, walter is an instinctive, virile and impulsive person and is happy with what nature has made him. However, she tries to put down all that was instinctive within him. She talks religion and philosophy to him, and in the process destroys him both as a father and as a social being. Afterwards, Mrs. Morel applies her standards on her two sons and never allows them to have a sound, constructive life. William dies young and Paul suffers her operations all through.

Paul is passionately devoted to his home——despite the presence of the erring father——to his mother, brothers, sisters, to literature and to the beauties of nature which he is to paint. It is in this context that west defines "the relation of Mrs. Morel and her son (as) an embroidery on the text."[46] In the complex web of relationships Paul chances to feel affinity with Miriam Leivers. The relationship can be defined as deep and spiritual in quality though Paul cannot sustain it beyond a measure. His relationship with Miriam fails to reach a satisfactory emotional adjustment. The main factor responsible for failure is that Miriam is too intelligent to appreciate much that is emotional. She only wants to possess Paul spiritually but has nothing physical to return. In all, their relationship is marked by the alteration between love and hate which is symbolised by the swing that advances to a point and then moves backward and so on but is makes no progress. Atmost immediately after beeaking with Miriam, Paul enters into a passionate sexual attraction for Clara Dawes. Clara's love for Paul is only flesh-deep and she hopelessly lacks intellectual and spiritual depths.

and Paul's soul could not be kept steady. Consequently, Paul turns away from her in disgust, just as earlier he had turned away from Miriam. Clara goes back to her husband and settles where she belongs. One thing may be emphasized here——Paul's experience with Clara serves as the training ground for a satisfying experience when the integration of flesh and spirit is ever to take place in his life.

(3) CONFLICT

Like the dimensions of Lawrence's vision that constitute the very fundamental textural inner logic of his writings, and the web of relationships that forms the weft of the total design, the phenomenon of conflict constitutes one of the most vital elements of the structure of *Sons and Lovers*. This point of the inter-connectedness of all the elements of structure in *Sons and Lovers* in reference to conflict is confirmed by Arnold Kettle who emphasizes that "Lawrence sees human relationships essentially in terms of conflict."[47] In point of fact, conflict manifests itself at the very root of life and hence establishes "the living conjunction between the self and its context."[48] Since conflict is fundamental to life, the existence of contrary forces in life is necessary to human existence. For this very reason Lawrence insists on both "the fact of opposition and the necessity for its existence."[49]

In *Sons and Lovers*, the conflict is multi-dimensional and so pervasive that it conditions the struggle of most of the characters to realize themselves in the circumstances they are placed. The conflict in the mind of Mrs Morel results in the conflict between her and Walter. Gertrude Morel is married in a family below her parental rank. To make up that gap she wants to culture her family but then she is confused about the concepts of culture and civilization. This conflict in her mind brings misery to all concerned in catastrophic dimensions. The husband gets alienated and caught in unrelenting conflict. children suffer from complexes and she too has her share of suffering. Mrs. Morel's conflict deepens with the coming of children and worsens as they grow up. After her alienation with the husband she dominates the affections and aspirations of the sons. Mrs. Moral interferes with the emotional life of the sons and causes internal schism in their character. Open criticism of Gyp by Mrs. Morel creates inner strain in William's mind which results in his death. The same motif is repeated in case of Paul when he comes into contact with Miriam and owing to multiple conflict the relationship never fructifies. Regarding Paul's relationship with Clara the mother fears the mystery in her character and discourages Paul. Sooner than expected the relationship ends the way it had ended in case of Miriam.

Paul's conflict is at once connected with his Mother's tension as also with that of Miriam and Clara. His conflict oscillates between normal desires and unconscious fixations and between love and hate in the affair with Miriam and Clara. After his Mother's death, Paul's conflict gets connected with the very question of survival. Miriam's conflicts are highly complex in nature and magnitude. Her conflict is throughly revealed in the observation that she "almost fiiercely wished she were a man and yet she hated men at the same time."[50] This fundamental trait continues throughout her relationship with Paul until both of them, victims as they are of conflict peculiar to them, realise their dangerous limitations :

> "He thought he was too sane for such sentimentality, and she thought herself too lofty."[51]

Thus, Miriam's conflict never allows her to be better than a swing that oscillates but never makes any progress. Like the other characters, Clara Dawes too partakes of her share of the phenomenon called conflict. Clara's relationship with Paul is purely physical but Paul, caught in the cocoon of his complex conflict, regrets that Clara does not give him wholesome love. She cannot give Paul anything of the sort for two main reasons that are rooted in her conflict——(2) She cannot understand the essence of sex that it can be anything beyond physicality and (2) because she suffers from the inescapable conflict as to why did she desert her husband. Confused as Clara is about her position and role in life, she manifests complex behaviour, and the "sense of mystery about her", as Mrs. Morel points out, will ever remain "hidden from every body."[52]

(4) Structural Orientation in Scenes and Characters

The fourth feature of structure in *Sons and Lovers* is oriented in the inter-play of scenes and characters. All the major characters are torn and tossed by conflict. The element of conflict is reflected in their hectic activities which, in turn, help develop the various threads of the story just as the scenes and incidents complement the onward movement of the plot. It is remarkable that the struggle of the characters and the complementing role of scenes and incidents gets vitally connected with such other aspects of the novel's structure as inner logic, inter-personal relationships, conflict and the symbols.

As a character, Mrs. Morel is linked with all the major characters in the novel, be it Walter, Paul, Miriam or Clara. Qualitatively, her character is constantly operative and recurrent. Her pervasiveness emanates from her misnomers that are the off shoots of her mis-conceived mission to culture her family. Although her aim is to bring about cultural transformation of her family yet she never moves beyond tinkering with the process of civilization. This misunderstanding about the very nature of her mission leads to multiple conflicts not only in her life but also in those of others. Similarly, Paul, like his mother works as a common chord between different characters. The qualities of Miriam are such that the single essence of her character: "On the whole——(she) scorned the male sex"[53] goes on recurring all through. And, it is on the strength of this that Miriam gets connected with all——with clara in matters of emotional link, with Paul and with Mrs. Morel in as much as both she and Clara are discouraged by her regarding their links with Paul. Such is the web between all the characters in the novel that they look like beads on the same string.

Evidently, the characters in Lawrence are dynamic and play their role with all the flexibility needed in the shaping of the novel's structure. In a latter of 5 June 1914 to Edward Garnett, Lawrence clarified his basic concept of characterisation :

> "The characters fall into the form of some other rhythmic form, as when one draws a fiddlebow across a fine tray deliberately sanded, the sand takes lines unknown."[54]

It is perhaps these likely unknown lines, in at once the totality and individuality of characters, that get connected with all the fundamental features of structure in *Sons and Lovers*. And, it is within these lines that the characters find delineation and acquire significance in the structure of the novel.

Structurally, there exists an inner logical coherence between the different chapters, scenes and incidents and the characters which form, in consonance with each other, a unified structure. In *Sons and Lovers*, all the chapters are long, and each contains many episodes and incidents linked to one another as on a necklace, each merging almost un-noticed into the next. If we have even a cursory look at the total structure of the novel, in essential terms, it is magnificant in its parts. No one would wish to be without the quarrel scene between the disaffected husband and wife (chapters I and II) ; the splendid tale of Paul collecting his fathers's wages or the scene of the children's games (Chapter II) ; the sad story of William's courtship and death (Chapter VI) ; Paul's walks in the country with Miriam (Chapter VII) and the painful scene of their parting (Chapter XI) ; the interaction between Panl and Clara (Chapter XII) ; the agony and death of Mrs. Morel (Chapter XIV). Still further, each and every appearance of Walter Morel casts a new light on the atmosphere, even though we may not always choose to accede to the author's moral judgements. These scenes cover not only the different curves in the plot of the novel but also either refer to or connect thematic developments with the dynamics of various characters in the novel.

(5) Symbols

Very much like the other four structural elements, discussed in the preceding pages, Lawrence has used symbols to unveil and show the inner texture of the structure of his novels. In *Sons and Lovers*, he has used mainly (I) Basic Symbols (indicating mutually opposed *qualities* of objects and humans) ; (2) Nature symbols and (3) descriptive symbols through characters.

Lawrence sees the phenomenon of inter-personal relationships and conflict (the two mutually opposed forces) symbolically. He so visualizes in terms of the elements of the dark and the light, the eagle and the dove, the tiger and the lamb, or the lion and the unicorn. All this comes under the category of Basic Symbols. That is why Lawrence shows the play of conflict in human life but also points to its resolution in the state of counter-poise. He so visualizes the mutually opposed forces in nature as a symbol because his ideas and art insist on "both the fact of opposition and the necessity for its existence."[55] Lawrence turns this into a regular dialectics. The lion and the unicorn would both cease to be, if either of them really won in the fight (for the crown) which is their sole reason for existing. This phenomenon is reflected in the various symbols when they are studied as an element of structure and it operates through characters, their activities and the scenes through which the plot moves forward. The symbol of the pollen-filled lilies is very effectively used in the structure of *Sons and Lovers*. Mrs. Morel rebels against the life-force and hates the child she carries with her. However, when Walter bolts her out of the house, and she is pacing up and down in the garden, she is struck by the pollen-filled lilies. In that situation she had the opportunity to be close to nature and rejoice in their fecundity. Symbolically, the scene dramatically reveals that Mrs Morel, in rebelling against the life-force, is cutting herself off from the source of vitality. In the same way, the symbol of the ash tree is effectively employed to show the complementary effect of the dark and sinister aspects of life. It heaves and shrieks when the parents indulge in quarrels and the hapless young childern are crouching in their room apprehending the worse to come. At the Leivers Farm, the feeding of the hen by Paul, and hesitance on the part of Miriam, the sudden appearance of the stallion in the woods are some of the major nature symbols that help represent human experience forming into the novel's structure. A similar role, in the structure of the book, is played by the symbolism of the coal pits that stand for the irrational principle of life that is particularly associated with Walter Morel.

Besides these, there is the crucial symbol——the Swing. It is expressive of the conflict in the mind of Miriam and a pointer to Paul that Miriam is not at all a dynamic person. More significantlv the Swing symbolises the persons and objects, which despite acttion and activity, never make any advancement. Evidently, the Swing oscillates——moves forward to a point, then moves backward but never makes any progress.

In this way, Lawrence has made a very copious use of symbols in *Sons aad Lovers* and the whole organisation is illuminating without being obtrusive. In view of the successful use of symbols in the structure of his novels, Aldous Huxley has highlighted, in his 'Introduction' to the *Letters of D.H. Lawrence* that "Lawrence was always a inescapably an artist."[56] In all, the art of Lawrence in structurr lies where the old world ends and the new begins to manifest "the disintegration of continuity of random events."

References

1. Harry T. Moore, *The Life and Works of D.H. Lawrence*, p. 154.
2. W.W. Robson, "D.H. Lawrence and Sons and Lovers", *The Modern Age* (Harmondsworth : Penguin Books, 1961), p. 292.
3. Frank Kermode, "Lawrence and the Apocalyptic Types," *Casebook Series on D.H. Lawrence*, p. 209.
4. Middleton Murry, *Reminisnces of D.H. Lawrence*, p. 167.
5. Anthony West, *D.H. Lawrence, the Novelist Series* (London : Arthur Barker, 1957), p. 73.
6. Ibid., p. 104.
7. Philip Hobsbaum, *A Reader's Guide to D.H. Lawrence*, p. 50.
8. Kenneth Young, *D.H. Lawrence* (British council Pamphlet), p. 12.
9. Michael Buter, *Passing Time*, trans. Jean Steward (London : Routledge 8 Kegan Paul, 1965), p. 143.

10. D.H. Lawrence, "Mornings in Mexico and Etruscan Places", *The Explicator*, XVII, (*iii*) (1925), p. 17.
11. Harry T. Moore ed., *The Collected Letters of D.H. Lawrence*, p. 105.
12. Ibid., p. 826—7.
13. Ibid., p. 511.
14. Eugene Goodheart, *The Utopian Vision of D.H. Lawrence* (Chicago : Chicago Univ. Press, 1963), p. 39.
15. E.M. Forster, Aspects of the Novel (London : Penguin Books 1970), pp. 93—94.
16. Jeremy Howthorn, *Studying the Novel* (London : Edward Arnold, 1985), p. 53.
17. Ibid., p. 56.
18. Keith Sagar, "Introduction", *Sons and Lovers* (London : Penguin Books, 1981), p. 11.
19. *Sons and Lovers*, p. 492.
20. James T. Boulton ed., *The Letters of D.H. Lawrence* (Cambridge : Cambridge Univ. Press, 1979), p. 466.
21. Ibid., p. 476.
22. Ibid., p. 517.
23. R.P. Draper ed., *D.H. Lawrence : The Critical Heritage*, p. 58.
24. Ibid., p. 68.
25. D.H. Lawrence, *Reflections*, p. 183.
26. D.H. Lawrence, *Women in Love* ed. Charles Ross, p. 164.
27. *Sons and Loverss*, p. 211.
28. D.H. Lawrence, *Fantasia of the Unconscious*, p. 91.
29. *Sons and Lovers*, p. 68.
30. Ibid., p. 239.
31. Ibid., p. 240.
32. D.H. Lawrence, *Aprocalypse*, p. 16.
33. Harry T. Moore, *The Collected Letters of D.H. Lawrence*, p. 179.
34. *Sons and Lovers*, p. 43.
35. Ibid., p. 46.
36. Ibid., p. 84.
37. Ibid., p. 200.
38. Ibid., p. 203.

39. Ibid., p. 242.
40. Ibid., p. 192.
41. Ibid., p. 340.
42. Ibid., p. 192.
43. Ibid., p. 325.
44. Anthony West, *D.H. Lawrence*, *The Novelist Series*, p. 146.
45. *D.H. Lawrence : A Collection of Critical Essays*, p. 16.
46. Anthony West, *D.H. Lawrence*, *The Novelist Series*, p. 114.
47. Arnold Kettle, *An Introduction to the English Novel*, p. 104.
48. D.H. Lawrence, *The Symbolic Meaning*, p. 117.
49. D.H. Lawrence, *Reflections*, p. 3.
50. Ibid., p. 204.
51. Ibid., p. 213.
52. Ibid., p. 324.
53. *Sons and Lovers*, p. 192.
54. *The Letter of D.H. Lawrences*, p. 201.
55. D.H. Lawrence, "The Crown." *Reflections*, p. 3.
56. Aldous Huxley ed., *The Letters of D.H. Lawrence* (London : Heinemann, 1956), p. 71.
57. Frank Kermode, *Critical Quarterly*, X (Spring 1968), p. 11.

□□

6

The Autobiographical Element

There is an array of critics right and left who emphasize that Lawrence's *Sons and Lovers* is an autobiographical novel ; an autotherapy about his early life. In point of fact, critical opinions abound in harping on the view that *Sons and Lovers* presents the story of Lawrence's life upto the death of his mother. Harry T. Moore qualifies the novel under discussion as "a kind of self-administered psychoanalysis". I David Daiches describes Lawrence as a disturbing writer adding that he forces the reader to question his own life :

> "You cannot simply accept his vision of life as...illuminating...you are compelled to apply it, to use it, to test it, to wonder about it".[2]

Elisco vivas probes Lawrence's work on theoretical basis, in an aesthetic context, and eventually traces the failures of his art back to subjective factors".[3] Besides Harry T. Moore, David Daiches, and Eliseo Vivas, the assessment of Lawrence's genius by W.W. Robson is rooted in the view that Lawrence is "not always objective or impersonal enough an artist, or that he occasionally violates the canon of aesthetic distance in his novels...or on some static conception of what a novel is, or ought to be".[4]

Adverse criticism also emanates from looking at a quotation half way. For example, a small part of a quotation by F.R. Leavis is lifted at random and on the legless strength of that the critic is misquoted. In that context, it has been pointed out that *Sons and Lovers* is an autobiographical novel because "something like a direct involvement of the author is evident."[5]

The fact, however, is that Leavis had not even referred to *Sons and Lovers* in his detailed observation, of which these words (quoted above) form only a part. His comment is reproduced as under :

> "The novels that succeeded *Women in Love* are not achieved enough to be wholly impersonal works of art because something like a direct involvement of the author is evident in them."[6]

The novel referred in the context——*Women in Love* itself was published in 1920 and *Sons and Lovers* much earlier in 1913.

Certain critics take it for granted that *Sons and Lovers* is pure autobiography and get lost in making irrelevant observations. Keith Sagar has argued that the charge against Lawrence is that consciously or unconsciously, he distorted the story of *Sons and Lovers* in order to make Paul and his mother come out of it better than they should, at the expense of Miriam and his father".[7] Probably at the time of writing *Sons and Lovers*, Lawrence had not realized the extent to which his mother had been in the wrong, and had been responsible for both the failure of her own marriage, and Paul's inability to make a satisfactory relationship with any other woman. On the face of it, there appears quite some truth in this charge. But the amount of weight it carries will depend very much on whether we read the novel as autobiography or fiction. Now, if we judge *Sons and Lovers* as autobiography, and know the facts, we can easily catch Lawrence lying ; but what is great imaginative fiction if not the telling of lies which are truer than facts. Alternatively, we have to ascertain as to what extent he was trying to write a novel with a more general relevance and significance. In point of fact, and by any balanced measure, the book is highly fictionalised in tone and texture, And studied objectively, it becomes evident that *Sons and Lovers* dramatises the transformation of known material into the fabric of art. It is in regard to this process of transformation that Graham Handly makes an apt observation : "Using the tools to hand, time worn tools to proven worth, Lawrence fashions with them something new".[8]

The totality of personal traits in Paul Morel and circumstances in his home and around have many close resemblances with those of D.H. Lawrence. Very much like Paul Morel, Lawrence too was a tortured soul both in personal life and in the social context. Both were prone to accept and reject things sharply, and hence suffered intensely. The atmosphere in Lawerence's home, like that of Paul, was embittered by the ceaseless bickerings of his parents in whose life enjoyment of conjugal felicity was a rare episode. In either case, repelled by the coarse brutality of the father and deep frustration in the married life of the mother, both...Lawrence as well as Paul] mutually developed deep emotional attachment with their female parents. Consequently, both of them grew, in whatever degree, into self consicous neurotics and could never succeed in establishing healthy and abiding emotional relationships with other women.

Besides these close resemblances in the personal traits and family circumstances, on the whole, the Morel family is closely modelled on the family unit of D.H. Lawrence. Gertrude Morel is Lydia Lawrence, nee Beardsall (1851–1910); Walter Morel—Lawrence's father is Arthur Lawrence (1846—1924); William [Morel—is Lawrence's elder brother William Ernest (1878–1901); Annie Morel ..Lawrence's sister, Ada who lived upto 1948 and had married Edward Clarke in 1913; Paul Morel . is David Herbert Lawrence (1885—1930); Lawrence's eldest brother, George, does not have a counterpart in the novel. Miriam Leivers——Jessie chambers, later Wood, who has left her own account of her relationships with Lawrence in *D.H. Lawrence : A Personal Record* (1935); Clara Dawes——Alice Dax, wife of Harry Dax, an Eastwood pharmacist. She was a feminine suffragette.

Like Lawrence's family (where the father is a Collier), the Morel family lived in a cottage situated on Greenhill Lane : "There lived the colliers who worked in the little gin–pits two fields away".[9] The description runs further : "And the cottages of these coal miners...formed the village of Bestwood".[10] In earlier drafts of the novel, Lawrence used real place names—— The Bottoms, was the Breach, Bestwood was Eastwood. The close resemblance in the naming of places in real life confirms the tinge of autobiography in *Sons and Lovers*. But then, rather comment on the point of the incidental parallelism in the two families and the identicality in the names of places, in either case, it is important to concentrate on the processes of literary creation and the consequent reality. And, in the context of literature the general principle is : Judge how the artist works on his own emotions and reactions in the process of creation. In case of *Sons and Lovers*, the novelist can be seen translating deeply experienced feelings into a moving human record. Middleton Murry has defined this creative exercise as "an index of his inner suffering, flrustrations and emotional complexes. They are all in the nature of personal revelations, some more, some less."[11]

Still further, a close biographical resemblance is sought to be established between Lawrence and Paul Morel, the second son of Gertrude and Walter Morel who has many of his creator's characteristics in him. Like Lawrence himself, Paul is different from his brothers and sisters right from his birth. Perhaps one aspect of the fact sought to be established is exemplified by the baby's action when his mother holds him up towards "the crimson, throbbing sun".[12] Besides this, Lawrence, like Paul Morel had a flair for art and painting. There is a reference in *Sons and Lovers* to this effect that at the age of twenty four Paul "worked a great deal from memory, using everybody he knew. He believed firmly in his work."[13] Much is made out of this reference to emphasize that this textual narration amply points to the autobiographlcal element in *Sons and Lovers*.

Details in the novel show how Gertrude Coppard, a woman of principle and breeding steps down into a working-class world and has little satisfaction in her own life. In one of his letters to R.A. Taylor, Lawrence describes his mother as a clever and ironical woman with an aristocratic descent who married beneath herself. Lawrence's father has been described as being a warm and hearty person who had an unstable temperament. He had no regard for principle, deceived his wife and drank heavily with the result that his wife showed contempt for him. This resulted into friction between them. The father was treated as a stranger in his own home. The children trembled with fear in the presence of their father and there developed a bond between mother and the two sons——William and Paul. This bond can be best summed up as both filial and deeply emotional. The mother conditioned her children to regard drunkenness as a form of extreme moral degradation. And, the convivial and genial Walter Morel was forced to be "a brutal and coarse beast"[14] as he was subjected to systematic ostracism. In this context, it is evident that Walter Morel has almost identical traits with Arthur Lawrence, Lawrence's father.

There is yet another dimension to the resemblances of identicality between the world of the Morels and that of the Lawrences. Qualitatively, Dorrit Cohn looks at *Sons and Lovers* as "a roman a clef".[15] However, it is not a roman a clef type of writing. The roman a clef is the sort of novel (with a key) that can bc 'unlocked' given the right 'Key'——in other words one which refers to real people, places or events in disguised form so that once one realizes what the work is about, the hidden references all become apparent. *Sons and Lovers* is not of this type because Paul Morel has a lot in common with the real D.H. Lawrence. Then, the opening of *Sons and Lovers* strikes us far more impersonal in contrast to the opening of any other novel——may be one by Lawrence Sterne——proverbially tinged with his personal self. The narration of *Sons and Lovers* focuses our attention on to what is told rather than who tells or how :

> "The Bottoms' succeeded to 'Hell Row' Hell Row was a block of thatched, bulging cottages that stood by the brook-side on Greenhill Lane. There lived the colliers who worked in the little gin-pits two fields away."[16]

In the very opening paragraph of his 'Introduction' to Lawrence's *Sons and Lovers*, keith Sagar has referred to Jessie Chambers' book wherein "he (Lawrence) said that Borrow had mingled autobiography and fiction so inextricably in *Lavengro* that the most astute critics could not be sure "where the one ended and the other began."[17] Jessie Chambers has given us to know that from his subtle smile (she) felt he was wondering whether he might not do something in the same fashion."[18] This observation of Jessie Chambers is highly suggestive and points to at least two things ——that one will speak or write what one knows and second (that) a writer creates something new and artistic out of what he knows.

Obviously, the elaborately expressed opinious in the foregoing pages that *Sons and Lovers* presents Lawrence's early life, cannot be accepted as Gospel Truths. Therefore, we must analyse this novel from the more open, and visibly more objective perspective. Though every novelist must, in some way, draw deep on his own experience yet, to hold on to such opinious is to be unjust to Lawrence, and that too when Lawrence had become almost notorious in some people's eyes for helping himself fictionally to the characters and fortunes of others. As a conscientious person, Lawrence was his own most sensitive critic. He was to go much further than conflating novel and case history. May be, in some subtle sense, he had been experiencing some difficulty in reconciling a sharp sense of his own life's experiences with the claims of art. However, on balance of judgement, it becomes evident that in *Sons and Lovers* he has successfully shaped "experience into a satisfactory work of art."[19]

If we just open out conceptually, then, in a broad sense, all "literature is the autobiography of humanity. Imaginative literature focuses, as nothing else can, the important elements that comprise the life of man."[20] In this regard Lawrence has handled the autobiographical element in *Sons and Lovers* remarkably and in virtue thereof the book "became a manifesto for a whole generation of young people in England."[21] Lawrence was wide awake that very often he was being subjected to injustice even by those persons who did not understand his philosophy and art. He has referred to one such instance in his letter of 20 May 1929 to Middleton Murry :

> "We don't know one another...if you knew how little we know one another! ...Believe me, we belong to different ways of consciousness."[22]

After Lawrence's death, Murry acknowledged the truth of this observation in his *Reminiscences* of *D.H. Lawrence* (1933), admitting that he had "never faced the real Lawrence",[23] and that he found it difficult to understand Lawrence's ideas. Lawrence has suffered incessantly due to inadequacy or carelessness in people's understanding of his ideas in the intended perspective.

May be, Paul Morel can be compared with D.H. Lawrence especially in regard to the so-called prototype of his mother. Like Lawrence, Paul seems to have the embryonic awareness that she had damaged him, broken his father, and given his beloveds no chance, yet he never very much says like Lawrence, that "all self-righteous women ought to be martyred."[24] In case of Lawrence, it may be a fact that Lawrence had started hating his mother but in *Sons and Lovers*, the worst that Lawrence makes Paul, inter-alia, say is :

> "My mother was wrong and I thought
> she was absolutely right."[25]

On the contrary, Paul continues to be devoted to his mother even after she had died. After her death, Paul is left a 'derelict' and, as it appears, "everything seemed to have gone smash."[26] In sum, for him the relationship between Paul and his mother stands for the essential paradox of all mother-son relationships.

Lawrence has protested against any attempt to call *Sons and Lovers* as an autobiographical novel. He has strenuously denied the charge :

> "It is an adaptation from life,
> as all art must be."[27]

We have yet another evidence about the high fortunes of *Sons and Lovers* rather than its being an autobiographical novel. In 1916, Edward Garnett, the publisher friend of Lawrence, and a very sagacious and straight—speaking person, wrote his assessment of *Sons and Lovers* and compared it, as a family epic and social history with Balzac and Flaubert :

> "This novel is really the only one of
> any breadth of vision in contemporory
> English fiction that lifts working class
> life out of middle-class hands, and

> restores it to its native atmosphere of
> hard veracity."[28]

This point needs to be clearly stated that Lawrence did not set out to write his novels in order to convince the readers of the truth of his own beliefs or ideals. Rather, it was Lawrence's conviction that no one has the right to impose his ideals on another person, for that is ideal bullying, which is the most hateful of things.

The biographical approach is fraught with problems and has involved many sharp debates. With a view to avoid any un-necessary indulgence, D.H. Lawrence advised : "Never trust the artist. Trust the tale."[29] And "generations of critics have pointed out that novelists can be very bad guides to their own work."[30] Let us agree, may be in the interest of satisfying certain egos that the autobiographical narration is, infact, one of the matrices of *Sons and Lovers*, and Lawrence hopelessly fails as an artist due to the biographical involvement. However, his achievement and "greatness", as Forster points out, "lies...upon something aesthetic."[31] Moynahan's book, *The Deed of Life : The Novels and Tales of D.H. Lawrence* (1963) studies "Lawrence's major works of fiction as works of art."[32] According to Lawrence, perfect art is a lie because it is perfect only when abstracted from "that context by which and in which it exists as truth."[33] As such, the novel, if it is really a work of art, contains no didactic absolutes ; and even if the artist or the novelist sets out to point a moral, the tale as a whole points the other way. It is in this context that Lawrenee recommends trusting not the artist, but the tale :

> "Let me hear what the novel says. As
> for the novelist, he is usually a dribbl-
> ing liar."[33]

Properly seen, we find that moral judgements are implict in Lawrence's novels, in that they supply the imaginative evidence for whatever judgements are made, and that Lawrence does let the novels speak for themselves. In one sense, Lawrence was deeply religious. He once said : "One has to be so terribly religious to be an artist."[35] Lawrence acknowledged that he wrote because he wanted men and women to change, and have more sense. And, what is autobiographical about it when just in that very context he observes :

> "Art must give a deeper satisfaction ....The degree to which the system of morality, or the metaphysic, of any work of art is submitted to critism within the work of art, makes the lasting value and satisfaction of that work."[36]

It was, once again, in this very context that Lawrence was both an artist and a prophet at once, and his moral intention and his art are inextricably bound up together. To bring them together, to join them was, in fact, Lawrence's declared intention. He says in his essay "Surgery for the Novel...or a Bomb":

> "It seems to me it was the greatest pity in the world, when philosophy and fiction got split. They used to be one, right from the days of myth. Then they went and parted, like a nagging married couple....So the novel went sloppy, and philosophy went abstract dry. The two should come together again...in the novel."[37]

It would be most appropriate to say that in Lawrence's novels whatever is moral is expressed in artistic terms, and all his artistic effort is meant to be moral. If his novels have a message, the novels themselves are that message. And so, E.M. Forster rightly called Lawrence a "prophetic novelist"[38] and the only "way to deal with prophets who are also artists" says Graham Hough, "is to respond to their art."[39]

According to Maurice Beeke, Lawrence belongs to the tradition of writers who feel that "the richness of a work of art may be measured by the completeness and intensity of the felt life manifested in the work."[40] In the same way, Dorothy Van Ghent has commented, with an even measure of a balanced judgement that Lawrence's "peculiarly intense" senstivity emerged as creative "passion for order."[41] In the estimate of Seymour Betsky the basic material may have been selected from closest autobiography while the book eventually remains "a successful novel (and) not a case history."[42] Lawrence has stated it in unequivocal terms that the novel is "an adaptation from life, as all art must be"[43] but by no stretch of imagination can these words be taken to imply that the adaptation is from the writer's own life. Judged in this context, *Sons and Lovers* is a work of art and not a case history for all the fact that Lawrence has worked the book through experiences selected from his life.

Reference

1. Harry T. Moore, *The Life and works* of *D.H. Lawrence*, p. 101.
2. *The Novel and the Modern World*, p. 178.
3. Eliseo vivas, *The Art of Peversity* ed., Kingsley Widmer (Seattle : Univ. of washington Press, 1962), p. 203.
4. Yudhistar, *Conflict in the Novels of D.H. Lawrence* (Edinburgh : Oliver and Boyd, 1969), p. 2.
5. F.R. Leavis, *D.H. Lawrence : Novelist*, p. 147.
6. Ibid, p. 147.
7. Keith Sagar, 'Introduction', *Sons and Lovers* (Penguin, 1981 p. 10.
8. Grahaim Handley, *Brodie's notes on D.H. Lawrence's sons and Lovers* (London : Pan Educational, 1967), p. 10.
9. *Sons and Lovers*, p. 35.
10. Ibid, p. 35.
11. Middleton Murry, *Between two Worlds* (London : Jonathan Cape, 1935), p. 71.
12. *Sons and Lovers*, p. 74.
13. Ibid, p. 364.
14. Edward Nehls, *D.H. Lawrence : A Composite Biography* (Wisconsin Univ. Press, 1957), p. 11.

15. Dorrit Cohn, *Transparent Minds : Narrasive Modes for Presenting Consciousness in Fiction* (Princeton : Princeton Univ. Press, 1978), p. 82.
16. *Sons and Lovers*, p. 35.
17. Jessie Chambers, *D.H. Lawrence : A Personal Record* (CUP, 1980), p. 110.
18. Ibid, p. 110.
19. Phihip Hobsbaum, *A Reader's Guide to D.H. Lawrence*, p. 51.
20. Harry T. Moore, *The Life and Work of D.H. Lawrence*, p. 246.
21. Martin Green, *The English Novel in the Twentieth Century*, p. 61.
22. *Collected Letters* II, p. 1154.
23. *Reminiscences of D.H. Lawrence* (London : Cape, 1933), p. 26.
24. Earl and Achsah Brewster, *D.H. Lawrence : Reminiscences and Correspondence* (London : Secker and Warburg, 1934), p. 255.
25. Frieda Lawrence, "Not I But the Wind" (Landon, 1935), p. 52.
26. *Sons and Lovers*, p. 481.
27. Jessie Chambers, *D.H. Lawrence : A Personal Record* (Cambridge : CUP, 1980), p. 204.
28. R.P. Draper ed. *D.H. Lawrence : The Critical Heritage* (London : Routledge and Kegan Paul, 1970), p. 117.
29. D.H. Lawrence, "The Spirit of Place," *Selected Literary Criticism* (London : Mercury Books, 1961), p. 297.
30. Jeremy Hawthorn, *Studying the Novel : An Introduction* (London : Edward Arnold, 1985), p. 78.
31. E.M Forster, *Aspects of the Novel*, p. 147.
32. *The Deed of Life*, p. XIII.
33. *D.H. Lawrence, Phoenix*, p. 475.
34. D.H. Lawrence, *Sex, Literature and Censorship*, p. 80.

35. *Collected Letters*, I, p. 189.
36. D.H. Lawrence, *Phoenix*, p. 476.
37. Ibid, p. 520.
38. *Aspects of the Novel*, p. 146.
39. Graham Hough, *The Dark Sun*, p. 5.
40. Maurice Beeke, "The Artist Theme," *Casebook Series* ed., Gamini Salgado, p. 177.
41. Dorothy Van Ghent, *Twentieth Century Views on D.H. Lawrence*. p. 15.
42. Seymour Betsky, "Rhythm and Theme", *Casebook Series*, p. 130.
43. Jessie Chambers, *D.H. Lawrence : A Personal Record* (Cambridge : CUP, 1980). p. 110.

□ □ □

7

Art of Characterisation

(A) GENERAL

In the general run of feeling and thinking characters in Lawrence have been given denominations quite arbitrarily or on the slightest and hastily formed impression. This approach needs to be corrected for understanding Lawrence's mind and art in the right perspective. Many lay readers and specialist evaluators have pointed out that in Lawrence's novels, characters act as mere mouthpieces for the novelist. Secondly, it is alleged that the reader is not left free to decide for himself. It seems, he is forced to side with certain characters, and against others for whon the novelist appears to have nothing but unjustified contempt. Another set of critics has pointed out that Lawrence's Characters suffer from inarticulate, taciturn and paralysing self-consciousness. But seen in the proper context these complaints, however widespread, are sure to be found only imaginary. In the year of the publication of *Sons and Lovers* (1913) there appeared an unsigned review in *Standard* that looked at the novel in an objective light :

> "In revelation of Character, Mr. Lawrence shows that he is a master and...any reading of the book shows the mark of genius.... No other English novelist of our time has so great a power to translate passion into words, but that is neither the beginning nor end of his art."[1]

Seen in this clear light, character may well seem to be one of the least problematic terms but a discussion is needed for its proper appreciation. In a novel, "We learn of character...

not direct (as in the theater or in the cinema) but mediated through a particular telling, a narrative source."[2] So, characters are those people who do things in a total context ruled over by some port of connective logic such as chronology, cause-and-effect, or whatever so that they come to be placed in an environment.

There are four major methods of characterization in fiction ——(2) By description or report (2) By action (3) Through thought or Conversation and (4) through symbol or image. As regards the first, in Conrad's *Heart of Darkness,* we come to know a very large amount of information about Mr. Kurtz before he ever appears before us. Other characters talk and report on his actions and beliefs that we feel as if we had met him ourselves. Secondly, action reveals much more than words. There is a well-known example in Turgenev's *On the Eve* (1859) when Insarov throws the insolent German into the water. It is an action of which his effete Russian companions are palpably incapable. From this action we learn something about Insarov which pages of description could not give us. Conversation and thought form a wonderful way of revealing a character. In Jane Austen's *Emma* we learn a lot about Miss Bates merely through her Conversation. Modern novelists such as James Joyce and virginia woolf have shown how we can learn about a character merely by following one's thoughts. In *Mrs Dalloway*, Clarissa Dalloway and Peter Walsh actually do very little, but by the end of the novel we feel that we know them quite well just by following so many of their thoughts. Fourthly, a novelist can use symbol or image to reveal and develop a character. In Lawrence's *Women in Love* (1920) one of the characters throws stones into the water at night to shatter the image of the moon. The intentions of the character throwing stones into the water symbolise his inner destructiveness. In *Sons and Lovers* (1913) the virginal Miriam is associated with white roses, whose "white, virgin scent" makes Paul feel "anxious and imprisoned,"[3] while the more passionate Clara is given red carnations, which splatter their petals over her clothes and the ground when she and Paul first make love. In the estimate of Forster what is valuable about Lawrence cannot be put into words. To present his characters Lawrence employs such of the usual stock-in-trade of the novelists as colour, gesture and outline in people "but evolved by such a different process that they belong to a new world."[4]

Lovers of literary creation and sociology are aware that around the year 1907 "great chnnges...were either occuring or pending both in English society and in the English novel".[5] D.H. Lawrence, like James Joyce, Ford Madox Ford, Gertrude stein and Joseph conrad, was at work on the innovation and experimentation front. Just as Lawrence stood apart from others in the handling of ideas and concepts, he was exclusively different in regard to the art of characterisation. Regarding his art of characterisation, Lawrence clarified his convictions and method in a letter of 5 June 1914 to Edward Garnett who had his own concepts regarding characterisation :

> "I don't think the psychalogy is wrong : it is only that I have a different attitude to my characters, and that necessitates a different attitude in you....I say, don't look for development of the novel to follow the lives of certain characters : the characters fall into the form of some other rhythmic form, as when one draws a fiddlebow across a fine tray deliberately sanded the sand taks lines unknown."[6]

In case of Lawrence, the convention of the omniscient narrator goes through the process of being, as it were, and the essence of narrations gets absorbed into the internal consciousness of several characters in turn. Raymond williams has observed recently of Lawrence that "in him as never before in the English novel, the language of the writer is at one with the language of his characters."[7] And while this instinctive atoneness with his people has undoubtedly given Lawrence the abilíty to open up to us great new areas of experience, the method may put a very real strain. However, this strain is worth it.

From the foregoing discussion, it is evident that the act of characterisation in Lawrence was ever in the process of refinement and growth. Toward the conclusion of his review of *Sons and Lovers* in the *Manchester Guardian*, Lascelles Abercrombie has observed that Lawrence has unique quality of illuminating both the obverse and reverse sides of his characters simultaneoushy and secondly he highlights the scope and variety of the life through "his insights into character" and therein lies his "achievement of the first quality."[8] According to Moore "there is always flux in Lawrence, always transition, always struggle, always renewal ; the life of his people is never undynamic."[9] And with these people, through their advanced consciousness— — heightend by their conflict and suffering—— Lawrence presents another type of character not always obviously similar to the realistic literary kind most readers are used to. But we look beyond the luminous flesh of these characters, to their beating consciousness, we find that they are not 'unreal', not mere mock-ups for the points of philosophy the author wants to put across. Lawrence could skilfully handle characters in the traditional manner but in *Sons and Lovers*, one of the finest tradition-type British novels— —he "developed an interest in matters beyond characteristion. Here and thereafter he did not fill his novels with dummies and corpses. Rather he illuminates fiction in a new way, and in dealing with ultra-sensitive people on the edges rather than in centres of life, he was giving his readers a new vision of existence."[10]

□□□

(B) MAJOR CHARACTERS

(1) Mrs. Gertrude Morel

(2) Walter Morel

(3) Paul Morel

(4) Miriam Leivers

(5) Clara Dawes

(1) Mrs. (Gertrude) Morel

The very first impression left on the reader is that Gertrude Morel, nee coppard belongs to the class of Destructive Women. However, an objective and closer study of her personality shows that she is a simple, gullible person with an intense ambition. Despite her inherent duality, Mrs. Morel has a deep sense of concern for her family, especially the two sons and is eventually discovered to be a woman of fortitude.

Mrs. (Gertrude) Morel is a gullible person with no shade of cunning about her. A superficial reader looks on her as a cunning, cruel and self-centred woman. Any impression formed on these lines by general reader is understandable. But it is difficult to concile when no less a critic than Moynahan insists on the impression that "Mrs Morel should not have dehumanized her will".[11] However, such an impression is rooted in some deep misunderstanding. As a matter of fact, right from the early stages, Mrs. Morel is all-believing by temperament and leads a life of instincts until she is unwittingly gripped by intellectuality. Before their marriage, Walter describes himself to be a mining contractor and she believes him. On his part, Walter is also strictly true, since a mining contractor was the official term for butty. The first time he returns home from work, she fails to recognize him. She thinks he is a negro. Afterwards, she tries to civilize him but fails. Therefore, she thinks of a simple way to set things right. She conditions her children to regard drunkeness as a form of extreme moral degradation.

Surfacially seen, Mrs. Morel looks to be in love with artificialities—absorbed in childish notions of things and ideas. For example "she enjoyed a kind of aristocracy among other women of the 'between' houses"[12] as she had the end (corner) house and then because her rent was five shillings and six pence instead of five shillings a week. Further, the fact that Gertrude belonged to a well-to-do family, cannot be lost right of. Her father had been a Nottingham Lace manufacturer and it was natural for her to grow class-conscious in that money oriented society. Owing to many adverse circumstances, she is obliged to marry beneath her family and therefore also it is quite natural for her to show off to satisfy her ego. Again, very few readers tend to realise that Mrs. Morel is a grace-loving, relig ious-minded lady. It has been well said of her :

> "Mrs. Morel was one of those naturally exquisite people who can walk in mud without dirtying her shoes".[13]

Mrs. Morel was religious by nature. In contrast to Walter, who preferred the public house, to Mrs. Morel the Chapel was like home."[14]

The second aspect of Mrs. Morel's character relates to her intense ambition, which is, in effect, an extension of herself. Cherishing and maintaining her ambition is something positive about Mrs. Morel. But to comprehend this situation one needs to have a close look at the whole situation that impelled her to stick to her ambition. Her father had been a Nottingham Lace manufacturer though ruined by an industrial slump. She marries beneath her partly because she has lost her marriage portion, partly because a tentative engagement to a scholarly young man has fallen through. When she comes to the village of Bestwood to live with Walter Morel she leaves a large city in touch with the great. World for a narrow, spiritually and economically impoverished mining community dominated by traditional codes effecting all areas of life from child care to the manner in which a collier divides his time, and money, between the pub and the home. She tries to adapt herself, but is soon put off by the uncouth slackness of her husband. Exasperated by the utter incompatability of her husband and the censequent failure to culture her family made her a bit dry and snobbish and obliged her to pursue her ambition through her two sons.

Meanwhile, Mrs. Morel's assertion of "superiority in station" among her neighbours "was not much consolation"[15] to her. Despite the "resolute bearing"[16] of the rather small woman of delicate mould called Mrs. Morel, there was a sense of loneliness, darkness and hopelessness. A choking sense of failure in the realisation of fondly-cherished ambition is qualified by Mrs. Morel in one of her terse expressions : "I wait, and what I wait for can never come."[17] So, impelled by the multiplicity of adverse circumstances Mrs. Morel does her best to realise her keen ambition to culture her family through her sons. In this regard, she deliberately participates in the lives of her sons whose future was her only hope :

> "Now she had two sons in the World. She could think of two places, great centres of industry, and feel that she had put a man into each of them that these men would work out what she wanted ; they were derived from her, they were of her, and their works also would be hers."[18]

Besides this, she likes to discuss philosophy and religion with Mr. Heaton, the local congregational clergyman. Also, as a part of her intellectual activities, she joins women's Guild and sits at home preparing papers to read to them, much to the interest of her children. Mrs. Morel takes up all these things in pursuit of her ambition which she thinks is a totally healthy activity.

A series of failures in the process of culturing her family cause her to lead a life of duality which, in turn, multiplies her conflict. However, it is worth mentioning that Mrs. Morel is obliged to lead alternative lives out of deep concern for her sons——William and Paul. Initially, William, the eldest son, is the focus of her attention ; wishes to see him grow to betterment and happiness. She was careful even about small matters. For example, she protects William from Walter's wrath after a neighbour's complaint. Secondly, she shuts Morel out of the family life, but only with a terrible and conscious fixity of purpose. Infact, she alienates Walter in the interest of her sons lest they should be spoilt by his bad example :

> "She was afraid of her son's going the same way as his father."[19]

However, she never ignores Walter un-necessarily. For example, when Paul wins a prize she insists on telling his father. Undoubtedly, she inflexibly pursues the right course for her children but feels some deep connection with her husband. Once tempers run high between Walter and William. William wants to attack his father but the mother discourages him. On enquiry she tells William that she cannot bear any affront by the sons against the father. In this way, Mrs. Morel's loyalty to her husband essentially continues. It is significant to note that for all the dislike she has for Walter, she loves the children by him ; rather feels "tied to him."[20] In a drunken states when Walter was troubling him, she calls him a "clumsy drunken fool"[21] but never really discards him, his brutalities notwithstanding.

Once again, Mrs Morel's attitude to Gyp, Miriam, and Clara is governed by her supreme concrn for her sons. superficially seen, it appears that Mrs Morel is one too many for Miriam Leivers on all occasions, and Clara goes in some awe of her. But, in point of fact, she adopts such a posture only to ensure the best for her two sons. Mrs Morel is very happy when William obtains a position in London with a shipping firm. In this, as in other matters, she was "very proud of her son".[22] But she is extremely depressed when William becomes infatuated with Gyp, a socially pretentious girl. She discourages him and deplores his financing of his fiancee. In case of Paul, Mrs Morel takes even greater precaution. Though herself in a state of serious illness, she wins Paul back from Miriam in an almost hysterical outburst in which she acknowledges that she never really had a husband. Mrs Morel wants Paul to grow like his father who had iron constitution. She wishes that her son falls "in love with a girl equal to be his mate... educated and strong"[23] However, when Paul developed a liking for Clara Dawes, she "prayed and prayed for him that he might not be wasted."[24]

Finally, Gertrude Morel appears to us as a woman of fortitude and is eventually discovered to be well-meaning. She is a person of dauntless and daunting character. And owing to this quality of her peronality she is considered superior by her neighbours. She could quell her husband by sheer strength of character except, of course, when he fails to know what he is doing. Economic circumstances, generally traceable to Morel's drinking habits, sometimes forces self-denial upon her and the children. But she never denies them her love and protection. The exceptional dimensions of Mrs. Morel's fortitude are revealed during the illness and eventual death of William. A telegram comes from William and it takes her to London where the son never recovers from pneumonia. It is with typical courage she does what she has to do in those tragic circumstances. Even the telegram she sends to her husband speaks of the strength, and of the tautness of her nature :

> "William died last night. Let
> father come, bring money."[25]

In point of fact, all the enforced economy, the habitual repression of feelings which has been her lot in life, are condensed into these few words.

Long mourning by Mrs Morel and the consequent negligence on the part of the mother lead to the serious illness of Paul Morel. As a matter of fact, it was Paul's illness, as his aunt rightly remarked, that saved Mrs Morel herself from the shock at the death of ther eldest son. In that situation she realised that she should have watched the living, not the dead. It is for Paul that she herself now lives. Similarly, she goes to Nottingham to see her husband when he is badly injured, and nurses him when he is unwell at home. Despite Walter's unlikeable attitudes, she "never quite wanted him to die. Still there was one part of her wanted him for herself."[26]

Mrs Morel gracefully endures the degradation of her intimacy with her husband and there is never any question of her breaking down under the pressure. On one occasion walter locks her out after he has come home drunk, and the spirit of the woman is powerfully conveyed as she walks in the garden :

> "Mrs Morel, seared with passion, shivered to find herself out there in a great white light...and gave a shock to her inflamed soul. She stood for a few moments helpless.

> ...then she got the air into her breast...while the child boiled within her."[27]

In yet another scene, Mrs Morel reacted with dignity and practical good sense. She has just been hit by the corner of a drawer flung by Morel. She receives a cut on the brow. The blood drips on Paul, and Morel watches until he finally breaks down. The only thing she said to walter was : "What of this child ?"[28] Fortitude against adversity is the basic domestic creed and it is clearly demonstrated in all crucial situations concerning Mrs Morel. Mrs Morel is down with serious illness but she pools up courage to nurse Paul back to health after he is severely beaten by Baxter. Her disease is in a far advanced stage but suffering greatly, in pain for much of her waning life, Mrs Morel, with characteristic courage and understatanding, tries to alleviate Paul's anguish on her account by underplaying her own agony :

> "Her eyes opened...and she looked at him pleadingly, almost wanting him to forgive her.... All the time she watched him lovingly. She was only sorry for him."[29]

As she was assuaging the feelings of others, on her own, she clings obstinately to life, as obstinately as she lived it ; and after her death the focus shifts from her to the watcher, Paul. As a Matter of fact, we see and know, as his mother wishes that she does indeed live on in Paul.

□□□

(2) Walter Morel

In a general estimate, it is often said about walter Morel that "he always ran away from the battle with himself"[30]. However, a close and objective assessment of Walter's personality reveals that besides his (1) physical attractiveness, and (2) devotion to drinks, he is (3) a victim of systematic alienation. In point of fact. walter is (4) a warm-hearted person who (5) deserves sympathy.

Though Walter Morel has been working in the coal pits from childhood yet he has a fascinating personality. He is naturally charming and virile, and has a certain presence. This aspect of his character gives an immediacy of appeal denied to the conventional. Moreover. he is free from the inhibitions of, sophisticated society and this adds to his charm. When Gertrude coppard saw Walter at the age of twenty seven, she was simply hypnotised :

> "He was well set-up ... and very smart. He had wavy black hair... and a vigorous black beard that had never been shaved"[31]

For quite long after his marriage with Gertrude he continued to be a good looking man and "when he chose he could still make himself a real gallant".[32] Besides his physical acquisitions walter was capable of impressive humility. Then, he was skilled at many things. In the estimate of his wife he was "a remarkably handy man ... could make or mend anything".[33] Remarkably, Walter has love for music and pleasant whistling. He nearly always whisted hymns. He had been a choir-boy with a beautiful voice.... His morning whistling alone betrayed it."[34] In this way, barring his weakness for drinks, walter continues to be a good man all through. In this regard, Moynahan has rightly pointed out that walter was a gem of a person ; only he should not have hidden his injured feelings behind a shell of cynicism."[35]

Devotion to drinks is the second aspect of Walter's character. He is widely talked about as a sot and and is known as something of a ladies' man though Mrs. Morel is the last to find out. As the children arrive, so he turns away from his responsibilities, calculaling the weekly budget after he has set aside so much for drink. Over the course of his life he changes his pubs but not his habits ; sometimes he helps in a pub, sometimes he arrives home in a high good humour, sometimes he arrives truculent, dangerous, and violent. He unfailingly keeps to the company of drinking companious though outside his home.

Like all drunkards, walter is a compulsive liar. He does not hesitate to lie to Gertrude that he has "A good bit of money"[36] besides telling her that "the house he lived in, and the next one, was his own".[37] Mrs. Morel goes white to the lips as she comes to know that Walter lives in a rented house and has house-hold furniture with bills "still unpaid".[38] On knowing about his poverty and drinking habits Gertrude starts despising him and he begins "to neglect her".[39] Although he is very steady at his work but significantly, he cannot afford to "miss work owing to his drinking".[40] As a drunkard Walter is blab—mouthed, and due to his indecencies the authorities are hateful to him. However, he does "abuse the pit—manager"[41] whenever he thinks of a catharsis.

The third noticeable phenomenon in Walter's life is his gradual alienation from his wife and children. In the early stage of their married life, the couple is happy but gradually a moral scar is uncovered in the character of Morel which spreads as the years elapse. In all, Mrs. Morel feels deceived in her marital relations with walter. They were united in wedlock in the romantic heat of the moment but soon they realise how they are unlike each other. She wants to reform him but in seeking to make him nobler than he could be, she destroys him. Ever after the birth of Paul, she starts looking at Walter as only a part of her circumstances. Further, Mrs. Morel's attitude changes towards Walter after the discovery that he neither owns a house nor possesses any money. Meanwhile, Paul, as earlier William despises his father for his drunkenness, uncouth manners and for causing pain and misery to his mother. Walter feels neglected and, out of humiliation, becomes peevish. This leads to frequent hot exchanges dotted with violence. Walter's domestic habits, sometimes deliberately over-acted, are calculated to offend the refined or the sensitive. Consider, for example, his fierce and obdurate assertiveness to Mr. Heaton, the congregational clergyman he find taking tea with his wife ; his bullying shouts when the children make too much noise, his physical assaults on his wife when he is worse for drink. In fact, he never loses sight of the class-war between himself and his wife, an awareness which they both share, so that there is a bitter irony in Mrs. Morel's referring to him as "My lord,"[42] when he ordered her to wait on him as his wife and in his calling her "A nasty little bitch".[43] To Mrs. Moral, and his son although, Morel looks like the nuisance"[44] and the entire life looks so to walter, it is noticeable, too, how Lawence, in a convincing way makes Walter Morel gradually age and disappear from active participation in the affairs of the Morel family. Consequently, we begin to ask ourselves what has happened to the husband who was so positive, in the earlier history of the family.

In terms of manners and actions Walter Morel has been described as crude and rash but this kind of reading is only one-sided. To be fair to walter, he has a heart of gold. In a state of drunkenness he man call his wife "a nasty...bitch"[45] but essentially "he was very gentle"[46]. Walter Morel has genuine love for his sons although they never respond to it ; reason being their mother had so conditioned them. Though Morel back-slides the economic and moral responsibilities of life yet essentially, he is a warm-hearted lovable person. Consider his cobbling or his making of fuses, when the children are delighted to help him, or his telling of stories about the pit ; consider, too, his tenderness when Paul is ill. Still further, one remembers too his exciterment when William comes home for the first time at Christmas, his silent reception of the newsthat William is dead, and his refusal to "walk past the office where his son had worked",[47] or to go near the cemetry where he was buried. Walter is full of Warmth for Paul when he wins first prize at an exhibition at Nottingham castle. He shares Paul's joy in his moment of great triumph. Many readers feel that walter sentimentalised situations after her death and that was the final way with him to "dismiss her"[48] but very few realize that "the real tragedy went in Moral in spite of himself.[49] In as much as Walter was good at heart, he was more so when he was repentent. In a fit of drunkenness he bolted his wife out. After a lot of rapping for about an hour he woke up and as he saw Gertrude out in the moon night, "it dawned on him what he had done. His head dropped, sullen and dogged".[50] He could not face her out of shame and hurried back. After that objectionable deed Walter "was for some days abashed and ashamed".[51] It is another matter that he "regained his old bullying in difference".[52] He was an early bird and so considerate to Gertrude that did not disturb her in the early morning and prepared his breakfast with his own hands.

Fifthly and finally, Walter Moral deserves our sympathy. On a casual and superficial evaluation Walter Morel can appear to be a character who fails to win our sympathy. Walter's warm-heartedness and the pathetic human quality always entitle him to share our sense of sympathy. For instance, once, at a very late stage in his half-broken relationship with his wife, he saw the passion in her eyes she had had for him but on recalling how she had alienated him, walter felt shy, rather scarred and humble. Eventuallly he wanted to run away from it and he did. May be, he is morally frail, but he is never beyond our sympathy. This helpless situation of Walter is given a considered stress when his wife is taken seriously ill, and he comes to see her. Reaching there he feels that no body owned him and "he backed out bewildered"[53]. Walter deserves our sympathy all the more when people refuse to accept his sincerity. After his wife's death he tells her relatives that he always tried to be good to her. However, no one is prepared to believe him though he may have been thoroughly honest in his assertions. After his wife's death, Walter lay awake until Paul returned home very late. All this while the terrible moments of loneliness almost unmanned him. To his surprise Paul noticed how "his father looked so forlorn"[54] whereas he had always been a man without fear. In a situation like that, there can hardly be a man who is not moved to pity. Eventually, Paul must have realised that it always takes two people to make a wrong, particularity a wrong that lasts a life time. Though Paul's heart was with his mother, yet life undoubtedly taught him that a small corner of it belonged to the father who, incapable of self-discipline, was capable of warmth, kindliness and concern. In view of this depiction of the comprehensive personality of Walter Lawrence Lerner speaks highly of Lawrence's art of characterisation : "Lawrence hardly ever created a character more convincing, more coherent and more alive than he has done in case of Walter Morel."[55]

□ □ □

(3) Paul Morel

In broad terms, Paul Morel is characterised as an impulsive, sensuous, fickleminded neurotic who shows signs of maturity only towards the last stage of his role in the novel. However, a close and perceptive look into his personality reveals that he comes quite close to represent the autobtographical element in *Sons and Lovers* and is vastly devoted to his mother. Paul's character is further revealed through his relationship with Miriam Leivers and Clara Dawes, and finally his multiple conflicts find quite some resolution to the very existential question that activated his mined to search for the meaning of life.

It is a common place of critical observation that *Sons and Lovers* is an autobiographical novel and Paul Morel has many of Lawrence's characteristics in him. No doubt, Paul is the pivot around which the whole action of the story moves and quite like Lawrence himself he is an exclusive type of person in his home. As in case of Lawrence, so about Paul, it is evident that Paul is different from his brothers and sisters. And perhaps this fact about his personality is essentially exemplified by the baby's action when his mother holds him up towards the crimson, throbbing sun, for he lifts up his fist, and his mother is ashamed of her impulse to give him back again whence he came. After that experience, Mrs. Morel decides to call him Paul. In the preceding scene and in the total context Mrs. Morel is reacting against the sensual and irresponsible nature of her husband, and subconsciously recurring to the influence of her father, George Coppard. who draw near in sympathy only to the Apostle Paul. In point of fact, Paul acquires the nickname of "Postle", an ironic look at the origin of his own name and perhaps also at his character. All this situation of Paul is quite comparable to that of D.H. Lawrence himself. Like Lawrence, Paul has to look for work early in life around the age of fourteen. Like his creator, Paul was a finely made boy, with dark brown hair and light blue eyes. In terms of comparison with the novelist Paul's "face has already lost its youthful chubbiness"[56] when he was not even fifteen, Lawrence, quite like Paul, had a flair for art and painting. What is narrated by the omniscient author fully strikes the similarity between D.H. Lawrence and Paul Morel, Paul was— —

> "...gradually making it possible to earn a livelihood by his art. Liberty's designs on various stuffs, and he could sell designs for embroideries, for after—clothes, and similar things."[57]

It is worth observing that characteristion which has it roots in autobiographical actuality often bears the impress of abiding truth ; it is so with Paul. He is far from perfect as was Lawrence or any other human being. For example, many of his actions, particularly with Clara and Miriam, are undertaken in blind selfishness —— but he is never less than human. A list of character "points" would demonstrate little, for he has the melleable, vibrant reflexes which are felt rather than recorded. In any case, Lawrence has not re-created history, he has created fiction which is a fine piece of art, may be close to life where parallels can always be located.

Devotion to his mother is the second trait of Paul's character. Mrs. Morel felt very unhappy due to the high handedness of her husband. However, Mrs. Morel felt that, as a baby, he was trying to undeistand something that was pain. This feeling draws him very close to his mother. Then, Paul is a sickly and delicate child who constantly requires nursing and care. This necessity paves the way for his later intimacy with his mother, which comes poignantly after the death of William. His childhood is laced with incidents which show his possessive love of his mother and hers for him. He likes to help his mother in the home, and even when he is a young man courting Miriam the turning of the home—made bread is his responsibility. As a child he resents his father, and after his mother's death he despises Morel's sentimentalising of his wife. So subject is he in childhood to his mother's influence that he accepts her standards of judgement in everything. All put together, Paul's "soul seemed always attentive to hers"[58]. For the reason that

Paul's father troubled his mother, he wished :

> "Lord, let my father die....Let him be
> killed at pit".[59]

Once, Paul was laid up with an attack of bronchitis. He wanted to be away from his father because "his father's presence seemed to aggravate all his sick impatience".[60] On the contrary, Paul was devoted to his mother to the extent that he loved to clean her shoes, and "cleaned them with as much reverence as if they had been flowers".[61] At the same time, Paul was a little frisky and open-minded ; on occasions behaved like a silly child and once he called his mother "duffer of a little woman,"[62] and due to this quality of Paul, his mother also felt frequently that "he would kill her soul."[63] All said and done, he was so attached to his mother that after her death he would have gone her dark way had not his miner strength sustained him to stick to life and light.

Any account of Paul's character remains incomplete if it does not show the complexity of his relationship with Miriam Leivers and clara Dawes. He gets to know Miriam when he chanced to visit the Leivers in the company of his mother. Miriam is a religious minded, spiritual sort of girl but through the negative process of denial of the physical needs Paul becomes fully aware of the importance of sexual fulfilment. Miriam wants to possess Paul's son but has nothing to return on the physical level. Therefore, for Paul the real Miriam and the associated predicament, stand together ;

> "She was afraid he would not let her.
> ...It has through out been Paul who
> has insisted that she wants only his soul."[64]

Despite his disillusionment with Miriam, some frail connection lingered on with her because Paul "was nearly a religon to her."[65] Through persuation of his mother and through his own experience, Paul severed his relationship with Miriam. However, after his mother's death he visited Miriam to assess if he could gain security by marrying her. Even this last effort at a meaningful relationship with Miriam failed and Paul developed leanings towards Clora Dawes, a married woman. For sometime he achieved physical harmony with clara but very soon he felt that she too was an incomplete person. If Miriam was all spirit, Clara was nothing but body. Therefore, he made sincere efforts to bring about reconciliation between clara and her husband. This could be put down as a spurt of altruism which Paul was prone to display in human relationships. But what is important is that he genuinely meant to re-unite the couple and he succeeded in his mission.

The one significant aspect of *Sons and Lovers* is to depict the inner vitality of Paul Morel's nature and this artistic effort of Lawrence corresponds with the observation : "only shimmeriness is the real living".[66] After the death of his mother Paul is left a derelict ——with no one to turn to, no one to build a new life upon, and hc turns away into his white night of spiritual and emotional numbness :

> "Everything seemed to have gone smash for the youngman. There was nothing left."[67]

In such an intense experience of nothingness Paul comes to feel like dying but finally he decides not to give in. In point of fact, he chooses not to own that life had beaten him."[68] In his final resolution, Paul rejects the path to darkness, and turns quickly "towards the faintly humming, glowing town".[69] In this way, the ending of the novel shows that Paul Morel's nature does contain an intact core of vitality which is his freedom."[70]

□□□

(4) Miriam Leivers

In broad terms, Miriam Leivers is looked upon as a spiritual-minded girl with no adequate understanding of the physical side of human nature. This impression seems to reduce Miriam to a one-dimensional character. However, an objective probe reveals at least four characteristic features of her personality. These features include her rootedness in duality resulting into a perpetual muddle over the spiritual and the physical sides of life. Thirdly, Miriam suffers at the hands of Mrs Morel to the extent that she is rendered unfit for a life of fulfilment.

Miriam Leivers is essentially a house divided against itself. Lawrence uses the element of irony to show that Miriam is disgusted by, and recoils from, the fact of birth as a result of animal mating. This complex in Miriam's mind may be there due to inherent proclivities but mostly this is because of her training by her mother. Miriam's mother has made a confidante of her and given her a disproportionate view of the man/woman relationship. Even on an ordinary everyday level she is physically afraid. In point of fact, she is physically afraid of man, as is shown in the incident with Paul when they were on the swing. Strangely enough, Miriam imagined that she could love, like and marry Paul if she could become physically stronger than him :

> "Then she could love him...take care of him ..have him in her arms".[71]

In this way, Miriam becomes a dreamy and impractical girl greatly influenced by her mother's religious mysticism. Miriam's mother was in the habit of exalting every thing——even a bit of house work——to the plane of a religious trust, besides being possessive to an intense degree. On these very lines, Miriam's whole relationship with Paul turns on the need to possess him completely from the spiritual point of view, though not from the physical. It was because of this complex duality in Miriam that her relationship with Paul collapsed. Besides her own affairs, Miriams duality is perceptible in her decisions affecting the relationships of others. She hates Clara Dawes but maintains friendly relations with her. She knows the lower nature of Clara yet introduces her to Paul. After this, she watches Paul's behaviour to enjoy at his cost, in a self-smothering way and also ever-fearful that he may be tempted to forsake her in favour of Clara whose physicality had fascinated him.

The second feature of Miriam's character constitutes the muddle over the spiritual and the physical aspects of life. Miriam is a dreamy, impractical girl. She wants complete possession of Paul's soul. Paul has good feelings for Miriam's qualities of perception but does not allow her to pocket him. Ever since Miriam came to know Paul when he visited Willey Farm along with his mother, she was "a little resentful of... strangers"[72]. She was hyper sensitive to matters of physical love and the "intimacy" between Paul and Miriam went in an utterly...chaste fashion".[73] It is interesting to note that right at the age of twenty Miriam was "full-breasted and luxuriously formed"[74] but she was chiefly rooted in her spiritual concerns. In a very subtle manner, it has been indicated by Lawrence that Miriam is incapable of physical fulfilment——it is by describing her, or having Paul think of her, in terms of religious imagery. Then, there is a more powerful suggestion regarding Miriam's state of mind——She lay as if she had given herself up to sacrifice. Miriam can easily do without physical contact but Paul is only human, and he feels fascinated towards Clara who is all physicality. Slowly but steadily Paul stopped making any demands on Miriam and this attitude "put them apart"[75] instead of drawing them together. The relationship failed because Miriam came nowhere near the realisation that one's consciousness enters into flux with another in the moment of polarization. Infact, she stood nowhere in comprehending that "each individual.. in coming to life must somehow 'connect' others".[76]

Thirdly, Miriam's character is affected by the intervention of Paul's mother in the interaction between Paul and herself. Mrs Morel is extremely anxious about the well-being of Paul and cautions him regarding the dreamy and impractical nature of Miriam. She is thoroughly convinced that Miriam is a complex person and sticks to life on its one extreme. For example, she is keen to marry but revolts at the very thought of physical intimacy. At the same time, she "almost fiercely wished she were a man and yet she hated men at the same time".[77] Paul's mother has desired to intervene because Miriam fiercely wants to possess Paul to the total neglect of the physical. Mrs Morel judges Miriam as "one of those who will want to suck a man's soul out till he has none of his own left."[78] Mrs Morel feels instinctively angry with Paul for going so close to Miriam. Paul pleads with his mother but he only feels "hopeless between the two".[79] This hopelessness and helplessness of Paul is further revealed as we find him suffering from a sense of uncertainty at many levels. For instance :

> "He might have married her ; but his circumstances at home made it difficult, and, moreover, he did not want to marry."[80]

Eventually, Miriam's relationship with Paul did not fructify due to the effective intervention of Mrs Morel whose judgement about the imbalanced personality of Miriam is finally confirmed when he visited her once again after the death of his mother. In that situation Paul wanted to assess if he could gain social and emotional security in marriage with Miriam but he had to withdraw with the well-grounded impression that he would gain nothing meaningful through such a relationship.

Miriam could never have a life of fulfilment. It is generally said that Mrs Morel was responsible for tragady in the Morel family. However, it is sufficiently evident that Miriam does Paul more injury through her soul possessiveness and physical negation, than does his mother. She lives in spiritual self-communion far removed from the normal regions of experience. Paul was in search of a harmonious relationship but in case of Miriam he "saw it only as a Platonic friendship."[81] Miriam is vastly responsible for the failure of her relationship with Paul because she is too intelligent to appreciate much that is emotional : "Learning was the only distinction to which she thought to aspire".[82] Besides all this, Miriam felt sure that "she was perpared for the big things"[83] such as sacrifice and renunciation but was just not sufficient for the small day-life."[84] Just before final parting of ways with Paul, when after his mother's death, he visited her to seek probable security in marriage but she let the rich opportunity slip out of her hands due to sheer ignorance of the ways of human heart. She tactlessly urges Paul to make physical love to her when he least wants to because of his suffering over the loss of his mother. In this way, Paul discovers that Mirian is inadequate——unable to give him physical and emotional understanding that he needs. Just on the contrary, and naively enough, she "wanted to re-discover him, his position, what he was now".[85] Other things being equal, Miriam should have been able to have Paul as her own for life "in the novel's pen-ultimate scene when he was there for the takings'[86] but this proved to be the moment of final parting.

□ □ □

(5) Clara Dawes

Clara Dawes is introduced when *Sons and Lovers* is about half way through. After Mrs. Morel and Mirriam Leivers, she is the third major female character in the book. The prominent aspects of her character include (1) the element of duality (2) mystery (3) physicality and (4) eventual loyalty to her husband.

The first aspect of Clara's personality is essentially rooted in her duality. She is supposedly contemptuous of men but if she needs anything in life, then it is men——vital and virile. It has been lavishly described that

> "She had...a full mouth, with a slightly lifted upper lip that did not know whether it was raised in scorn of all men or out of eagerness to be kissed, but which believed the former."[87]

Another instance of Clara's duality is revealed through her conversation with Paul, which mostly hinges on Clara's bitterness about the status of women and the menial tasks to which they are subjected. Later, however, there occurs a meaningful episode which does much to explain Clara's attitude. Paul and Clara meet Miss Limb and become aware of her loneliness. She loves horses more than anything else in life. The fact about Miss Limb as also about Clara is revealed by Clara in an unguarded moment that Miss Limb's love for the animal was out of her need for a man. Initially, Paul and Clara appear to have no liking for each other since Clara had-scornful eyes."[88] Essentially, however, Clara's relationship with Paul contains, its main ingredient, her strong sexuality which can only mean consummation or separation. Clara has very much a will of her own, and resists for some time but she is vulnerable though she tries to hide the other side of her dual nature——she lives in some fear of being caught by a man again. It is mainly because of her duality that Clara is separated from her husband, Baxter Dawes, and has taken to rebellious ways to nourish the rights of women. The duality of Clara's character comes to be demonstrated further when Paul visits her for the first time at her home. Admittedly, she has the conventional concern as to whether where she lives is good enough, but the interior——mother and daughter at work, with the mother a strongly vocal character——shows how claustrophobic her existence is :

> "She spoke humbly to him. He had
> surprised her in her drudgery."[89]

Yet another instance of Clara's duality relates to the fact that she always regrets as to why she deserted her husband though she had deliberately separated from him.

Secondly, Clara looks to be a simple, straight woman yet there is an element of mystery about her. Looked at from a close quarter, one easily comes to know that she is not merely what she appears. A part of that mystery becomes perceptible in her preculiar dressing habits :

> "Out doors she dresssd very plainly,
> down to ugliness, indoors she always
> looked nice."[90]

In comparison to other girls at the place of her work, Clara did not very much mix up with her fellow-workers. All put together :

> "There was a sense of mystery about
> ...her....Her history was open on the
> surface, but its inner meaning was
> hidden from everybody."[91]

Another instance of her mystery relates to the fascinating fact that although Clara's husband was a wrestler yet owing to her formidable, otherwise amiable-looking personality her husband's "manner was of cowed defiance."[92] The mystery about Clara deepens as we come to know that her relationship with Paul is that of strong sexuality yet she cannot overcome the guilt in her leaving her husband. As in case of the earlier relationship, so also in case of Paul-Clara interaction Mrs. Morel tries to play a constructive role. Mrs. Morel is extremely conscious about the well being of Paul as earlier of William. In that regard, she provides Paul with standards of normally and wholeness by which she could judge both Miriam and Clara. After Paul developed a liking for Clara, she "prayed and prayed for him, that he might not be wasted."[93] Mrs. Morel apprehends harm to Paul mainly due to the in-built mystery in Clara's character.

An overwhelming sense of physicality to the total exclusion of spirituality, is the bane of Clara's character. If Miriam is an incomplete person due to her extreme, if not needless, spiritual orientation, Clara's relationship with Paul fails because she is all body and no soul. In essential terms, her relationship with Paul turns out to be purely physical and hence yields no meaningful satisfaction to either of them. Clara recognizes sex as a primary fact of life and the one vital source of guiding the course of human affairs but then she has no appreciation for spirituality. For some time, Paul and Clara evince mutual attraction towards each other because Clara possesses "a sort of fierceness in her"[94] and Paul loves her with the intensity of "a young animal."[95] The love scenes between Paul and Clara are shown as full of passion and flare. No doubt, both of them are gripped by what may be defined as physicality but, in the interest of the needs of art, Clara's reactions are not measured in the same detail as those of Paul. Eventually, they are disillusioned with each other vastly due to this element of physicality which proves at once inadequate and too much for them. If they are led to each other owing to each being strongly aware of the other physically, they also part company through realisation of the lack of essential spirituality in them, though particularly in Clara.

The fourth aspect of Clara's character relates to her sense of loyalty to Baxter Dawes. In point of fact, there is a tug of war between two forms of loyalties between Paul and Clara. Paul is tied to the chords of loyalty with his mother and Clara fails to subdue her guilt ridden conscience as to why did she leave her husband. Paul can never really give himself wholly to any woman, much less to Clara, while his mother is alive. What is significant is that Clara comes to realise this. Although they continue to have their moments of happiness——generally physical ones——Clara's guilt in having left her husband intensifies continually. In this regard Clara, inter-alia, feels, as we may imagine that she falls much short of Lawrence's dictum : "Think sexfully, honestly and completely."[96] Clara's feelings are heightened when she learns from Paul that Baxter has been very ill. Although before that, and even after Baxter has beaten Paul, she probably senses on the few occasions that the latter has taken his mother's advice and wants to get all of them out of his system. At this stage Clara comes to act courageously and tells Paul that she had Baxter more completely than she has had him, and thus becomes the second woman (Miriam was the first) to puncture his ego. Admitted that she does not fully understand Paul, she makes it quite clear that Paul does not understand her.

Above all else, one feels that Clara wants some kind of security, away from her mother, and thus she does not object when Paul manipulates her back to Baxter. In a sense, Clara feels that she has used Baxter ill. There is some rough idea of justice in this, for Paul too feels that he has mis-used Baxter, and the result is a reconciliation that exposes a certain type of human acceptance. May be, Clara looks down right practical after all that experience and she comes around to a way of thinking about Paul, seeing her husband as more manly because he owns that he is beaten whereas Paul will not. In point of fact, she knows now that she can rule Baxter, who is much bowed down but it also seems that she must end the injustice she has been doling out to him. And, therefore, she decides to join company with her husband.

In ultimate analysis, it becomes evident that both Paul and Clara have conflict peculiar to them and, interestingly, want its resolution through each other. Consequently, their relationship fails to confinue smoothly. Paul does not get wholesome, constructive love from Clara but the difficulty with Clara is that she does not understand the essence of sex. This mutually shared feeling leads to inner strain and eventually they part company. In this way, there is a natural, rather healthy end to Paul-Clara relationship since she went where she belonged. Clara "went with her husband to sheffield, and Paul scarcely saw her again."[97]

Reference

1. R.P. Draper ed., *D.H. Lawrence : The Critical Heritage*, p. 58.
2. Jeremy Hawthorn, *Studying the Novel*, p. 2.
3. *Sons and Lovers*, p. 210.
4. E.M. Forster, *Aspects of the novel*, p. 147.
5. Frank kermode, *Essays on Fiction*, 1971—82 (London : Routledge and Kagan Paul, 1983) p. 33.
6. *Lietters*, pp. 199—201.
7. Raymond Williams, *The English Novel from Dickens to Lawrence* (London : Chatto and Windus, 1970), p. 173.
8. R.P. Draper ed., *D.H. Lawrence : The Critical Heritage*, p. 68.
9. Harry T. Moore, *The Life and Work of D.H. Lawrence*, p. 245.
10. Ibid., p. 276.
11. Julian Moynahan, *The Deed of Life*, p. 22.
12. *Sons and Lovers*, p. 36.
13. Ibid., p. 166.
14. Ibid., p. 245.
15. Ibid., p. 36.
16. Ibid., p. 37.
17. Ibid., p. 41.
18. Ibid., pp. 143-44.
19. Ibid., p. 93.
20. Ibid., p. 40.
21. Ibid., p. 76.
22. Ibid., p. 90.
23. Ibid., p. 317.
24. Ibid., p. 317.
25. Ibid., p. 181.
26. Ibid., p. 83.
27. Ibid., p. 59.
28. Ibid., p. 77.
29. Ibid., p. 441.
30. Ibid., p. 79.
31. Ibid., p. 43.
32. Ibid., p. 54.

33. Ibid., p. 46.
34. Ibid., p. 53.
35. Julian Moynahan, *The Deed of Life*, p. 22.
36. *Sons and Lovers*, p. 47.
37. Ibid., p. 47.
38. Ibid., p. 47.
39. Ibid., p. 49.
40. Ibid., p. 52.
41. Ibid., p. 52.
42. Ibld,, p. 76.
43. Ibid., p. 98.
44. Ibid., p. 157.
45. Ibid., p. 98.
46. Ibid., p. 106.
47. Ibid., p. 187.
48. Ibid., p. 401.
49. Ibid., p. 401.
50. Ibid., p. 61.
51. Ibid., p. 63.
52. Ibid., p. 63.
53. Ibid,, p. 471.
54. Ibid., p. 470.
55. Lawrence Lerner, "Characterisation As Art," *Sewanee Review*, LXI (1965), p. 75.
56. *Sons and Lovers*, p. 129.
57. Ibid., p. 364.
58. tbid., p. 96.
59. Ibid., p. 99.
60. Ibid., p. 107.
61. Ibid., p. 166.
62. Ibid., p. 169.
63. Ibid., p. 245.
64. Ibid., p. 489.
65. Ibid., p. 340.
66. Ibid., p. 202.
67. Ibid., p. 481.
68. Ibid., pp. 483-484.
69. Ibid., p. 492.

70. Julian Moynaham, *The Deed of Life*, p. 29.
71. *Sons and Lovers*, p. 192.
72. Ibid., p. 169.
73. Ibid., p. 213.
74. Ibid., p. 272.
75. Ibid., p. 353.
76. Frederick R. Karl, *A Reader's Guide to Great Twentieth-Century English Novels*, p. 154.
77. *Sons and Lovers*, p. 204.
78. Ibid., p. 211.
79. Ibid., p. 246.
80. Ibid., p. 339.
81. Ibid., p. 224.
82. Ibid., p. 192.
83. Ibid., p. 271.
84. Ibid., p. 271.
85. Ibid., p. 486.
86. Julian Moynahan, *The Deed of Life*, p. 22.
87. *Sons and Lovers*, p. 237.
88. Ibid., p. 239.
89. Ibid., p. 320.
90. Ibid., p. 330.
91. Ibid., p. 324.
92. Ibid., p. 238.
93. Ibid., p. 317.
94. Ibid., p. 240.
95. Ibid., p. 325.
96. D.H. Lawrence, *Fantasia*, p. 325.
97. *Sons and Lovers*, p. 481.

SELECT BIBLIOGRAPHY

—Ada, Lawrence. *The Early Life of D.H. Lawrence*. London : Martin Secker, 1931.

—Aiken, Conrad. "Mr. Lawrence ; Sensationalist," *The Nation*. 12 July 1924.

—Aldington, Richard. *Portrait of a Genius, But*. London : Heinemann, 1950.

—............"A Wreath for Lawrence", *Encounter*. XVI, IV (April 1960).

—Alldritt‘ Keith. *The Visual Imagination of D.H. Lawrence*. London : Arnold Heinemann, 1971.

—Allen, Walter. "D.H. Lawrence in Perspective", *Penguin New Writing*. Autumn 1946.

—Alter, R. *Partial Magic : The Novel as a Self-Conscious Gence*. Berkeley : Berkeley University Press, 1975.

—Auerbach, Erich. *Mimesis : The Representation of Reality in Western Literature*, trans. Willard Trask. Princston : Princeton University Press, 1953.

—Balbert, Peter. *D.H. Lawrence and the Psychology of Rhythm*. Mouton, 1974.

—Bartlitt, Norman. "Aldous Huxley and D.H. Lawrence," *Australian Quartelly*. XXXVI. *i* April, 1960.

—Beal, Anthony ed. *Selected Literary Criticism*. London : Heinemann, 1956.

—Beebe, Maurice. "Lawrence's Saceed Fount : The Artist Theme of Sons and Lovers," *Texas Studies in Literatnre and Language*. IV, March 1964.

—Ben-Porat, Z. "The Poetics of Literacy Allusion," *A Journal For Descriptive Poetics and Theory of Literature*. I, April 1976.

—Bennet, Arnold. "D.H. Lawrence's Delusion," *Evening Standard*. 10 April 1930.

—Berne. E.L. *Games People Play : The Psychology of Human Relatianship*. London : Martin Secker, 1966.

—Blackmur, R.P. "D.H. Lawrence and Expressive Form," *Language as Gesture : Essays in Poetry*. London : Allen & Unwin, 1954.

—Bramley, J.A. "The Challenges of D.H. Lawrence," *Hibbert Journal*. April 1960.

—Brewster, Achsab. *D.H. Lawrence : Reminiscences and Correspondence*. London : Martin Secker, 1934.

—Bruss, E. "The Game of Literature and Some Literary Games," *New Literary History*. 9 March 1977.

—Bynner, Witter. *Journey with Genius : Recollection and Reflections Concerning the Lawrences*. London : Peter Nevill, 1953.

—Carswell, Catherine. *The Savage Pilgrimage*. London : Martin Secker, 1932.

—Carter, Frederick. *D.H. Lawrence and the Body Mystical*. London : Archer, 1932.

—Cavitch, David. *Lawrence and the New World*. New York : Rinehart & Winston, 1969.

—Chesterton, G.K. "The End of the Moderns," *London Mercury*. January 1933.

—Clarke, Colined. *Casebook Series on D.H. Lawrence's Sons and Lovers*.

—Clarke, Colin. *River of Dissolution : D.H. Lawrence and Romanticism*. London : Archer, 1932.

—Cohn, Dorrit. *Transparent Minds : Narrative Modes for Presenting Consciousness in Fiction*. Princeton : Princeton Univ. Press, 1978.

—Coombers, H. "D.H. Lawrence Placed," *Scrutiny* March, 1949.

—Coveney, Peter. *The Image of Childhood*. Peregeine, 1967.

—Cross, Barbara. "Lawrence and the Unbroken Circle," *Perspective*. X, 3 April 1980.

—David, Daiches. *The Novel and the Modern World*. Chicago : Chicago Univ. Press, 1960.

—Dehlberg, Edward. "A Literary Correspondence‘" *The Sewance Review*. 67 (1959).

—Daleski, H.M. The *Forked Flame : A study of D.H. Lawrence.* London : Faber 1965.

—Delavenay, Emile. *D.H. Lawrence : The Man and His Work ; The Formative Years—1885—1919.* London : Heinemann, 1972.

—Draper, R:P. *D.H. Lawrence, The Critical Heritage.* London: Routledge & Kegan Paul, 1969.

—............*D.H. Lawrence.* London : Routledge, 1975.

—Eastman, M. *The Literary Mind : Its Place in An Age of Science.* New York : Barnes 8 Noble, 1931.

—Eliot, T.S. "Son of Woman", *Criterion* July 1931.

—Fair, Judith (ed) *Twentieth Century Interpretations of Sons and Lovers.* Englewood Cliffs : Prentice-Hall, 1970.

—Ford, H. George. *Double Measme.* New York : Rinehart and Winston, 1965.

—Foster, Richard. "Criticism As Rage : D.H. Lawrence." A.D.H. Lawrence Miscellany," London : Heinemann, 1961.

—Forster, E.M. *Aspects of the Novel,* London : Penguin, 1972.

—Fox, Ralph. *The Novel and the People* : London : Lawrence and Wishart, 1979.

—Freeman, Mary. *D.H. Lawrence : A Basic Study of His Ideas.* New York : Grosset and Dunlop, 1955.

—Friedman, Alan. *The Turn of the Novel.* London : Oxford Univ. Press, 1966.

—Gamini, Salgado ed. *D.H. Lawrence : Sons and Lovers.* London : The Macmillan Co., 1969.

—Ghent, Dorothy Van. *The Engilish Novel : Form and Fuuction.* New York : Harper & Row, 1967.

—Gomme, A.H. ed. *D.H. Lawrence : A Critical Study of the Major Novels and other Writings.* New York : Barnes & Noble, 1976.

—Goodheart, Eugene. *The Cult of the Ego : The Self in Modern Literature.* Chicago : Chicago Univ. Press, 1968.

—...........*The Utopian Vision of D.H. Lawrence.* Chicago : Chicago Univ. Press, 1963.

—...........“Lawrence and Christ,” *Partisan Review*. XXXI, *i* (Winter, 1964).

—Gorden, David J. *D.H. Lawrence as a Literary Crittc*. London : Yale Univ. Press, 1966.

—Grant, Douglas “England's Phoenix,” *University of Toronto Quarterly*. XXVII (1958).

—Green, Martin. *The English Novel in the Twentieth Century*. London : Routledge & Kegan Paul, 1984.

—Gregory, Horace. *D.H. Lawrence : Pilgrim of the Apocalypse A Critical Study of D.H. Lawrence* : London : Martin Secker, 1934.

—Guttmann, Allen. “D.H. Lawrence : The Politics of Irrationality,” *Wisconsin Studies in Contemporary Literature*. VI (1964).

—Hardy, Barbara. *The Appropriate Form : An Essay on the Novel*. London : Athlone Press, 1964.

—Hinz, E.J. “The Beginning and the End : D.H. Lawrence's Psychoanalysis and Fantasia,” *Dalhousie Review*. L 11 (1972).

—Hobbrook, David. *The Quest for Love* : London : Methuen, 1964.

—Hobsbaum, Philip. *A Reader's Guide to D.H. Lawrence*. London : Thames & Hudson, 1981.

—Hoffman, F.J. *The Achievement of D.H. Lawrence*. Oklahoma, 1953.

—Hough, Graham. *The Dark Sun : A Study of D.H. Lawrence*. London : Gerald Duckworth, 1956.

—Hulme. T.E. *Speculations : Essays on Humanism and the Philosophy of Art*. London : Routledge and Kegan Paul, 1936.

—Hutchinson, Peter. *Games Authors Play*. New York : Methuen, 1983.

—Jarrett-Kerr & Martin. *D.H. Lawrence and Human Existence*. London : SCM Press, 1951.

—Jones, W.M. "Growth of Symbol : The Sun in Lawrence and Eudora Welty," *University of Kansas City Review*. XXVI (March 1987).

—Kazin, Alfred. "Sons, Lovers and Mothers," *Partisan Review*. XXIX, iii (1962).

—Kermode, Frank. Lawrence and the Apocalyptic Types," *The Critical Quarterly*, 10 (1968).

—...........D.H. Lawrence. London : Modern Masters, 1973.

—Kessler, Jasche. "D.H. Lawrence's Primitivism," *Texas Studies in Literature and Language*.

—Kettle, Arnold. *An Introduction to the English Novel*, Vol II. London : Arrow Books, 1962.

—Klingopulos, G.D. "Lawrence's Criticism," *Essays in Criticism*. 7 (1957).

—Krook Dorothed. *Three Traditions of Moral Thought*. Cambridge : Cambridge Univ. Press, 1957.

—Kuttner, A. Brook. "Sons and Lovers : A Freudian Appreciation," *Psychoanalytic Review*. III (1961).

—Lawrence, Frieda. *The Memories and Correspondence*. London : Heinemann, 1961.

—...........*Not I, But the Wind*. London : Chatto & Windus, 1971.

—Lawrence, D.H. *Fantasia of the Unconscious and Psychoanalysis and the Unconscious*. London : Heinemann, 1961.

—...........*Studies in Classic American Literature*. London : Heinemann, 1964.

—...........*Apocalypse*. Florence : G. Orioli, 1931·

—...........*The Symbolic Meaning : The Uncollected Versions*. Arundel : Centaur Press, 1962.

—...........*The white Peacock*. London : Heinemann, 1910.

—...........*The Teespasser*. London : Heinemann, 1912.

—...........*Sons and Lovers*. London : Heinemann, 1913.

—...........*The Rainbow*. London : Heinemann, 1915.

—...........*Women in Love*. New York : Grosset and Dunlop, 1920.

—............*TheLost Girl.* London : Heinemann, 1921.

—........ : *Aaron's Rod.* London : Peter Nevill, 1922.

—...........*Kangaroo.* London : Heinemann, 1923.

—...........*The Boy in the Bush.* London : Heinemann, 1923.

—...........*St Mawr.* London : Heinemann, 1925.

—...........*The Plumed Serpent.* London : Heinemann, 1926.

—...........*Lady Chatterley's Lover.* London : Duckworth, 1928.

—...........*The Virgin and the Gypsy.* Philadelphia : Centaur Press, 1925.

—...........*Mr. Noon.* London : Longman & Co., 1989.

—...........*Sex, Literature and Censorship.* London, Heinemann, 1957.

—...........*Reflections on the Death of a Porinpine and other Essays.* Philadelphia : Centaur Press, 1925.

—...........*Phoenix : The Posthumons Papers of D.H. Lawrence.* London :Heinemann, 1961.

—...........*The Letters of D.H. Lawrence*, ed. Aldous Huxley. London : Heinemann, 1956.

—Leavis, F.R. *D.H. Lawrence : Novelist.* London : Chatto & Windus, 1955,

...........*Thought, Words and Creativity : Art and Thought in D.H. Lawrence.* London : Chatto & Windus, 1976.

..........."Lawrence Scholarship and Lawrence," *Sewancc Review.* L XXI (1963).

—Lodge, David. *The Modes of Modern Writing : Metaphor, Metonymy, and the Typology of Modern Writing.* London : Secker, 1977.

—Lawrence, Lerner. *The Truth tellers : Jane Austen, George Eliot, D.H. Lawrence* London : Chatto and Windus, 1967.

—Miller, Nolan. "The Success and Failure of D.H. Lawrence", *Antioch Review.* XXII, 1968.

—Moore, Everett T. "D.H. Lawrence and Censor Morons," *Bulletin of the American Library Association.* LIV, 1960.

—Moore, Harry T. *The Achievement of D.H. Lawrence.* Norman : Univ. Oklahoma Press, 1953.

—......ed. *AD.H. Lawrence Miscellany.* Carbondale Southern Illinois Univ, Press, 1959.

—...........*The Intelligent Heart : The Study of D.H. Lawrence.* London : Heinemann, 1955.

—...........*The Life and Works of D.H. Lawrence.* London : Unwin Books, 1963.

—...........*The Priest of Love : A Life of D.H. Lawrence.* New York : Straus & Giraux, 1974.

—...........ed. *The Collected Letters of D.H Lawrence.* London: Heienmann, 1962.

—Moynahan, Julian. *The Deed of Life : The Novels and Tales of D.H. Lawrence.* Princeton : Princeton Univ. Press, 1966.

—Murry, Middleton, J. *Love Freedom and Society.* London : Jonathan Cape, 1957.

—...........*Between Two Worlds* : London : Jonathan Cape, 1935.

—...........*Reminiscence of D.H. Lawrence.* London : Jonathan Cape, 1933.

...........*Son of Women.* London : Jonathan Cape, 1931.

—Nehls, Edward. *D.H. Lawrence : A Composite Biography.* Madison : University of Wisconsin, 1957-59.

—Newman, P.B. "D.H. Lawrence and the Golden Bough," *Kansas Magazine.* XI (1962).

—Nin, Anais. *D.H. Lawrence : An Unprofessional Study.* London : Spearman, 1961.

—Niven, Alstair. *D.H. Lawrence : The Novels.* Cambridge, Cambridge Univ. Press, 1978.

—Panichas, G.A. *Adventures in Consciousness : The Meaning of D.H. Lawrence's Religions Quest.* The Hague : Mouton, 1964.

—Pinto, V. de S. *D.H. Lawrence, Prophet of Midlands.* Nottingham, 1951.

—Potter, Stephen. *D.H. Lawrence : A First Study.* London : Jonathan Cape, 1930.

—Raleigh, J.H. "Victorian Morals and the Modern Novel," *Partisan Review*. XXV, 1958.

—Read, Herbert. "On D.H. Lawrence," *Truth is More Sacred* London : Routledge and Kegan Paul, 1961.

—............"On D.H. Lawrence," *The Twentieth Century*. CLXV (June 1959).

—Rees. Richard. *Brave Men, A study of D.H. Lawrence and Simone Weil*. Gollanz, 1958.

—Rimmon-Kenan, Shlomith. *Narrative Fiction Contemporary Poetics*. London : Methuen, 1983.

—Roberts, Walter. "After the Prophet : The Reputation of D.H. Lawrence," *Month*. April, 1962.

—Robson, W.W. "Sons and Lovers," *The Modern Age*. London : Penguin, 1961.

—Rosenthal, T.G. "The Writer as Painter". *The Listener*, 6 September 1962.

—Sagar, Keith. *The Art of D.H. Lawrence*. Cambridge ; Cambridge Univ. Press, 1966.

—Sanders Scott, *D.H. Lawrencz : The World of the Major Novels*. New York : Vision, 1273.

—Schelling, T.C. *The Strategy of Conflict*. Cambridge : Combridge Univ. Press, 1960.

—Schorer, Mark. "Fiction with Great Burden," *The Kenyon Review*. XIV (Winter, 1952).

—Scott, N.A. *Rehearsals of Discomposure*. London : John Lehmann, 1952.

—Seligmann, H.J. *D.H. Lawrence : An American Interpretation* New York : Seltzer, 1924.

—Shoufield, Andrew. "Lawrence's other Censor," *Encounter*. XVII (September 1961).

—Smith, Glover F. *D.H. Lawrence The Rainbow*. London : Edward Arnold, 1971.

—Spender, Stephen. *The Creative Element : A Study of Vision, Despair and Orthodoxy Among Some Modern Writers*. London : Peter Nevill, 1953.

—Spilka, Mark ed. *D.H. Lawrence : B Collection of Critical*

Essays. Englewood Cliffs : Prentice Hall, 1963.

—............*The Love Ethic of D.H. Lawrence*. Bloomington : Indiana Univ. Press, 1955.

—............"Was D.H. Lawrence a Symbolist" ? *Accent* (Winter, 1955).

—............ed. *Towards a Poetics of Fiction*. London : Indiana Univ. Press, 1977.

—Stacy, R.H. *Defamiliarisation in Language and Literature* : New York : Rinehart and Winston, 1977.

—Tedlock, E.W. (ed). *D.H. Lawrence and Sons and Lovers*. New York : Univ. Press, 1965.

—Thomas, John Heywood. "The Perversity of D.H. Lawrence", *The Criterion*. 10, No 38, 1930.

—Tindall, W.Y. *D.H. Lawrence and Susan His Cow* New York : Columbia Univ. Press, 1939.

—Tiverton, Father William. *D.H. Lawrence and Human Existence*. Rockliff, 1951.

—Trilling, Diana. "A Letter of Introduction to Lawrence," *Partisan Review*.. XXV, i (Winter, 1958).

—Trilling, Lionel. *A Gathering of Fugitives*. Secker Warburg 1957.

—Traschen, Isadore. "Pure and Ironic Idealism in D.H. Lawrence", *South Atlantic Quarterly*. (Spring, 1960).

—Van Ghent, Dosothy. *The English Novel* : *Form and Function*. New York Rinehart, 1953.

—Vivas, Elisco. *D.H. Lawrence* : *The Failure and the Triumph of Art*. London . Allen & Unwin, 1961.

—Weiss, Daniel A. *Oedipus in Nottingham, D.H. Lawrence*. Seattle ; Univ, of Washington Press, 1962.

—Welch, Colin. "*Black Magic, White Lies*," *Encounter*. February, 1961.

—West, Authony. *D.H. Lawrence, The Novelists Series*. London : Arthur Barker, 1951.

—West, Paul. "D.H. Lawrence : Mystical Critic," *Southern Review*. XI (Winter 1965).

—Wheeler, M. *The Art of Allusion in Victorian Fiction*. London: Routledge & Kegan Paul, 1979.

—Wilder, Amos N. *Theology and Modern Literature*. London : Chatto & Windus, 1970.

—Worthen, John. D.H. *Lawrence and the Idea of the Novel*. London, Macmillan, 1970.

□ □ □

INDEX

L

M

N

O

U

V

W

Z

☐ ☐ ☐

57